DoD Architecture Framework

A Guide to Applying System Engineering to Develop Integrated, Executable Architectures

By Steven H. Dam, Ph.D.

SPEC
System and
Proposal Engineering Company

DoD Architecture Framework – A Guide to Applying System Engineering to Develop Integrated, Executable Architectures

Published by SPEC

P.O. Box 397

Marshall, VA 20116

www.spec-1.com

Use of Copyrighted Material

Vitech Corporation has allowed SPEC to use their copyrighted materials. Those materials have been identified as such in this book.

Trademarks

All terms mentioned in this book that are known to be trademarks or service marks have been appropriately capitalized. SPEC cannot attest to the accuracy of this information. Use of a term in this book should not be regarded as affecting the validity of any trademark or service mark.

Warning and Disclaimer

Every effort has been made to make this book as complete and accurate as possible, but no warranty or fitness is implied. The information provided is on an "as is" basis. The author and publisher shall have neither liability nor responsibility to any person or entity with respect to any loss or damages arising from the information contained in this book.

GPBU01991-00004

DoD Architecture Framework

ISBN: 1-4196-3296-5

Publication Date: March 20, 2006

Printed in the United States of America

Contents at a Glance

Introduction 1

Chapter 1: Why Do We Need a DoD Architecture Framework? 3

Chapter 2: What Is DoDAF Anyway? 11

Chapter 3: How Is DoDAF Being Implemented? 73

Chapter 4: What's the DoDAF Missing? 95

Chapter 5: What Makes a "Good" Methodology? 107

Chapter 6: How Does SE Provide the Architecture Views? 153

Chapter 7: How Can We Communicate the Results Better? 179

Summary 187

Author's Acknowledgements 189

Introduction

The term "architecture" means many things to many people. To a couple hoping to build a new house, it means the design of their home, usually, represented by drawings called "blueprints." To a landscaper, this means the plan for placing trees, shrubs, flowers, and other elements of an exterior design, which includes lists of specific plants. In addition, the smart gardener knows the environment (the context of the garden): drainage, where the sun is at all times of day, and the prevailing winds. To a database designer this can mean the physical schema used, which is often represented by series of class diagrams for each data object to be contained within the database.

In the world of Department of Defense (DoD) architectures, we take a different view of the word "architecture" than the ones above. Here, we are interested in the logical and physical descriptions of systems, and how they will interoperate. The ultimate goal is the generation of information for decision makers to determine what the proposed systems are likely to do, to compare these systems with related current and proposed technology, and to acquire appropriate new technologies compatible or complementary with current capabilities. In addition, developers need to know how these systems must perform in the operational environment to be acceptable and therefore procured.

The purpose of this book is to reach the worldwide DoD Architecture Framework (DoDAF) audience, including Government and contractor personnel, with the message that System Engineering is the key to developing architectures and that DoDAF only serves as a means of comparison. This book will help the users to understand the value and limitations of the DoDAF. We also make a case for *executable architectures*, which have been validated using modeling and simulation techniques. The need for executable architectures, not just drawings made in Microsoft PowerPoint, becomes obvious when we realize the potential cost savings of detecting an error early in the architecture phase, rather than later in the design, development, verification, and evaluation phases. The approach to architecture development that we recommend will lead to more complete and defensible architectures.

1

As the author, I, Dr. Steven Dam, bring over 30 years of software development and systems engineering experience, mostly at the system-of-systems architecture level. As part of an architecture development for the Defense Airborne Reconnaissance Office (DARO), which has been subsumed back into the Office of the Secretary of Defense (OSD), I participated in the development of version 2.0 of the C4ISR Architecture Framework, the predecessor to the current DoDAF 1.0. From that involvement, I observed the "original intent" of the Framework and how it has evolved over the past 7 years. From this perspective, I will present various "myths" about the Framework, both DoDAF and its predecessors.

In the time since the C4ISR Architecture was released, I have participated in a number of high level architecture developments, including the Financial Management Enterprise Architecture, Net-Centric Enterprise Services, and Future Combat Systems. Many of these activities are still on-going; so, the benefits of applying architecture to provide investment decisions are still new. Results are usually better assessed after some time has passed and more data about actual system performance collected. Therefore, history will judge the application of the DoDAF as a success or failure.

[handwritten marginalia: "and perhaps not yet known"]

[handwritten marginalia right: "(may provide)"]

This book could not have been possible without information gathered from other practitioners. As material presented in open forums, such as the annual IDGA Architecture conference, those materials have been referenced to provide full credit to the individuals who provided that information. We provide it here to enable the reader to be able to contact other practitioners who have contributed to the overall body of knowledge in architecture development.

This book was derived from the popular Systems and Proposal Engineering (SPEC) training course "SYS 501: Developing Executable Architectures Using the DoD Architecture Framework." The authors of this course are ~~myself~~ and Jim Willis, Colonel, USAF retired. Colonel Willis's background includes over 30 years in the intelligence, operations, and military training domains. He and I have worked on many of the architectures mentioned above.

We hope by the end of this book that you will be more familiar with the DoD Architecture Framework, have a better understanding of how to develop executable architectures, and make them compliant with the Framework. With this book and a little luck, you should have a more successful and pleasant architecture development effort.

1

Why Do We Need a DoD Architecture Framework?

Back in the late 1980's the problems with large architectures and systems became apparent; the interoperability among systems was so bad that soldiers had to use pay phones and other electronic devices from home to communicate with the Pentagon.[1]

The 1991 Gulf War highlighted the many difficulties of interoperability when we couldn't find the SCUDs, and many systems still didn't fully work together as planned. To fix these problems industry experts proposed a variety of architectural solutions. Unfortunately, these solutions came in many forms and formats. Even the information contained in each solution was different. This left the Government evaluators in a very difficult position; they could not tell the difference between architectures or the ways they related or supported each other. Hence, they needed a framework to determine the appropriate information content that would allow them to distinguish between the architectures. To accomplish this, as in most Government programs, they created the Architecture Working Group (AWG). The AWG was comprised of representatives from every command, service, and agency across the Department of Defense. Although they were intended to be representative of their particular organizations, these representatives brought their own perspectives. This approach is a natural difficulty with working groups, but a necessary one to make progress.

The product of this working group was C4ISR Architecture Framework 1.0 (see Figure 1-1). It was a new "standard." It provided a way in for architecture developers to compare their architectures to determine which was best. It was called C4ISR (command, control, communications, computers, intelligence, surveillance, and reconnaissance) because it was in this domain that interoperability was a major problem. It wasn't really a standard, because DoD had recently (circa 1993) removed the requirement for the military standards and

which may have exacerbated the interoperability problem. (handwritten)

---

[1] See article on the U.S. Operation Urgent Fury in Grenada, 1983 at http://www.globalsecurity.org/military/ops/urgent_fury.htm, accessed March 2006.

specifications. So, they provided this framework as guidance to the department not a mandatory standard.

Not long after they released version 1.0, the working group and their support contractor MITRE received thousands of comments and corrections from throughout DoD and its contractor community. As a result, the AWG began development of version 2.0 in 1996. I was fortunate to be asked to represent the Defense Airborne Reconnaissance Office (DARO), since I was working on developing their Vision Architecture.

To address all the comments, the AWG made a number of changes in creating version 2.0. Examples were added, because one of the overriding comments was that the "templates" for each of the products were too abstract. The panel members were asked to bring in various examples, and each product received a number of examples in different formats. The use of different formats was intentional to drive home the idea that the form wasn't the important characteristic. The information content and its supporting methodology were the point. The AWG intended that most knowledgeable, experienced practitioners would analyze the examples, recognize the similarities, and develop formats appropriate for representing and communicating their own architecture.

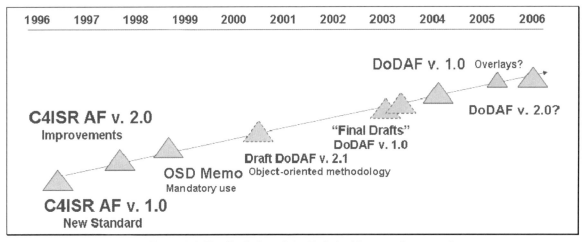

Figure 1-1. The Evolution of the DoD Architecture Framework.

Perhaps the most significant change was the recognition that architecture can be broken into three *views*: operational, systems, and technical (more on these views will be presented in the next chapter). In version 1.0, these three views were actually considered to be three different *architectures*. That change was significant, because it was the realization that the three views are highly dependent, overlapping, and not completely separate architectures. Unfortunately, this change has not been fully understood or embraced by all of DoD. For example, many of the Services have an Operational Architect, a Systems Architect, and a Technical Architect. Since we recognize that these views are highly interdependent, this means that the three different architects (and their organizations) must coordinate completely to ensure that the three views come together properly. As you can imagine, this makes it very difficult to obtain an integrated architecture, since any organization wants to have a level of autonomy from another.

We have seen this problem occur within major architecture programs as well. It seems natural to divide up the work by the work products. The results of the different efforts then must be integrated with the overlaps removed. We know that this usually makes integration difficult, if not impossible, without a tremendous effort. Hence, many of the major architectures use literally hundreds of people to conduct them and take years to complete. As a counterpoint, the DARO Vision Architecture, which had the stunning breadth of all airborne reconnaissance platforms and ground systems as part of its charter, was accomplished in a matter of months by no more than a dozen people. Many of those people had other jobs in addition to the architecture work. For the ground based infrastructure, which today forms the basis for the Defense Common Ground System (DCGS), Dr. David Craig, a brilliant engineer from MITRE, and I were the two primary contributors on the Vision Architecture. We captured the entire architecture in a system engineering tool (CORE) at six levels of decomposition in a matter of two months time. The rest of the study period (a year) was devoted to validating the architecture and briefing it around OSD and the rest of the community.

The DARO Vision Architecture was the first time I employed this tool, process, and technique on an architecture. We had used it for a number of years on Advanced Concept Technology Demonstration (ACTD) projects with great success. I will present this methodology in more detail in Chapter 5.

Not long after C4ISR Architecture Framework version 2.0 was released, OSD/C3I and the Joint Staff, J-6 committed to make use of the Framework mandatory for the C4ISR domain. Until that time it was guidance only. However, no directives, regulations, or instructions were changed subsequently, so the memo was no longer valid after six months. Some major users, such as the US Transportation Command (USTRANSCOM), even expanded the application of the Framework beyond the C4ISR domain to other areas.

Those of us on the panel knew that this was like any product developed by a committee; an incomplete set of compromises, but a good starting point. We knew there were many the things not included, such as metrics, costing, levels of hierarchy, and use of simulation. We anticipated that these would be resolved in version 3.0. However, a few other things got in the way.

First, we had the looming potential crisis embodied by the Year 2000 (Y2K) problem. For those who weren't part of "Y2K," this was a result of decades of code written for computers that were very memory limited.

Few people realized that the complex space systems that travel to and landed on the Moon had orders of magnitude with less memory than the modern pocket calculator. The result was that many programs assumed that only two digits were needed to specify the date (e.g., 59 would represent 1959, since it was assumed that the first two would always be "19"). That wasn't much of a problem until the calculations approach the turn of the millennium. If you wanted to determine how many years had elapsed between 1989 and 1959 the calculation would result in 30 (89 - 59). However, if you wanted to find the same thing between 2005 and 1985, the result would be -80 (05 - 85) and not 20 years as one might expect. Needless to say that could cause some very significant problems if the algorithms didn't handle the problem correctly (and many didn't).

DoD had come late to the Y2K party, as the insurance companies, elevator manufacturers, and others in the commercial sector had run into the problem as early as the late 1980s. DoD was very worried that major sensor and weapons systems, both strategic and tactical, could be affected, giving enemies an opportunity to strike. Fortunately, a crash effort was made and no major failures were observed.

After the Y2K problem passed, a number of drafts emerged from the team developing the Framework. One of the most interesting came in 2000. This draft included the option that Object-Oriented methodologies were valid ones for developing C4ISR AF products. Although the Framework explicitly said that any notation or methodology could be used, a number of people had begun interpreting the Framework to only allow diagrams similar to the examples shown in the document to be compliant. Since these products were all structured analysis diagrams (IDEF, Yourdon-Demarco, etc.), people assumed that you couldn't use the recently emerging Object-Oriented techniques that were used in software development.

Another interesting feature of this draft was the extension of the Framework to all of DoD, and hence, the tentative versioning: DoDAF 2.1. This changing of version numbers has caused some confusion. Many people don't understand why the versioning started with the C4ISR AFs wasn't continued, but applying it to DoD was a whole new way to look at the problem.

After a number of other drafts (of version 1.0) in 2003, the final version 1.0 was released on 09 February 2004. The documents are available at http://www.defenselink.mil/nii/doc/. The major changes from C4ISR AF v. 2.0 to DoDAF v. 1.0 are:

- Applies to all DoD
- Restructured: 2 Volumes and a Deskbook for implementation
- Product selection is based on the intended use of the architecture

- Removed "Essential" and "Supporting Products"
- Moves toward a data-centric approach, less oriented toward products
- Most of the examples have been replaced by the Deskbook
- Emphasis on "Capabilities," not requirements

We will discuss these and other changes in the next chapter.

Another change was the inclusion of "UML-like" diagrams, an example of which is shown in Figure 1-2.[2] The reason we say "UML-like" is that although they use some of the UML notation, such as the very unpopular stick figures, these diagrams do not show up in the UML specifications.

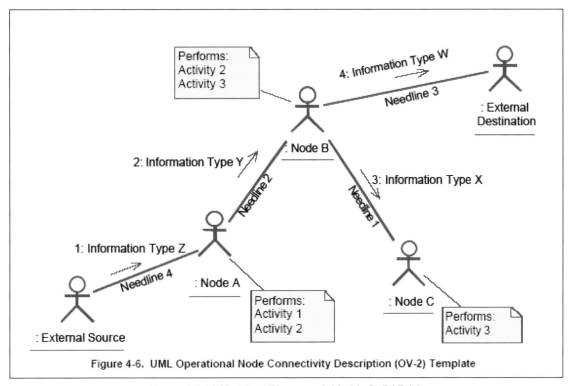

Figure 4-6. UML Operational Node Connectivity Description (OV-2) Template

Figure 1-2. "UML-Like" Diagrams Added in DoDAF 1.0.

In addition to the changes in the Framework itself, OSD has revised every major policy to include architecture products. The policies include ones related to fielded systems, as well as ones in the acquisition process, thus making DoDAF products *essential for funding all DoD programs*. OSD has also developed a data-centered architecture repository, called the DoD Architecture Repository System (DARS). It uses the Core Architecture Data Model (CADM) as the basis for export and import into DARS. We will discuss more on this in Chapter 5.

The bottom line on this new Framework is that while enhancing readability by: expanding the volumes; improving the text; and providing

---

[2] DoD Architecture Framework v. 1.0, 9 February 2004, Volume II, p. 4-11

insights into ways to employ the Framework (in the Deskbook). Otherwise, the Framework isn't a major change from the C4ISR AF 2.0. The product set remains essentially the same (some minor variations, which we will note in Chapter 2), it doesn't emphasize the need to develop your own methodology, and it implies that data alone (i.e. as captured in the CADM) is sufficient for architecture description.

The lack of new views, particularly ones that would better aid decision makers, provide some guidance on life cycle costing as associated with the architecture and a product that would recognize that architecture should drive the test and evaluation (T&E), and operations and support (O&S) processes. As such, it means that you, the architect, must formulate the results in other forms that will be more useful to the decision making process. As such, other frameworks and techniques may provide inspiration for improving communications, as discussed in detail in Chapter 7.

The lack of emphasis on the need for a methodology has caused quite a few of problems. Many practitioners assume that the Framework itself is a methodology or can easily be turned into one. The problem lies in the loose coupling of the products to any theoretical structure. Without a complete, consistent way to capture and represent the parameters of the architecture, you will likely not have a coherent, convergent solution, or set of potential solutions. This problem will lead to poor requirements for the system design and development. We know the effect of poor requirements in the past: reduced performance, massive program overruns, schedule slips, and even program cancellations – after billions have been spent.

The emphasis on a "data-centric" approach to architecture is equally disturbing. As in life, we are more than the sum of our parts. Architecture is about seeing the big picture, not just the data. I think by "data centric" the OSD personnel really mean that they want to get away from the "religious wars" between structured analysis and object-oriented zealots and tool vendors, as the depictions of the DoDAF products imply. Although I understand their desire, it's very difficult to actually accomplish. The attempt to make CADM the data model standard is flawed (as will be discussed in Chapter 5), and its clear OSD personnel recognizes it, since they have advocated a migration to the emerging AP 233 standard. The use of an international standard is clearly a good way to go. However, even this standard may not be complete enough to fully describe the underlying structures, which can only be visualized (the only time when a picture *is* worth a thousand words). Complex logic is best shown in a flow diagram, with logical constructs, such as "and" and "or." Trying to parse logic out of common English (or any other language for that matter) is very difficult, hence the need for "requirements analysis."

Although we highlighted the problems above, overall I think the DoDAF represents a significant step toward standardizing architectures within the department and outside with other U.S. organizations and coalition partners. The limitations noted above are relatively minor and easy to work around. For example, if you are working on an enterprise architecture, such as the Business Management Modernization Project (BMMP), you might want to look beyond the DoDAF for additional products to fill in the gaps. The Zachman Framework (show in Figure 1-3) provides higher level views (in the Scope primarily) that can aid in the development of a more complete, strategic architecture.

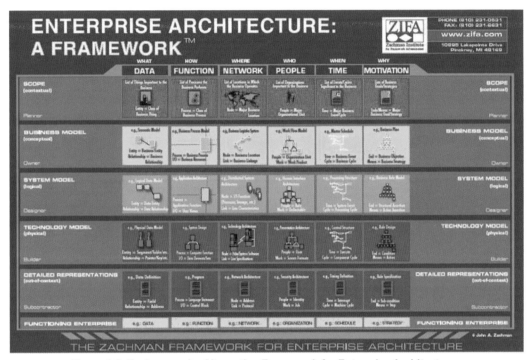

Figure 1-3. Zachman – An Alternative Framework for Enterprise Architectures.

Many of the ideas and concepts from Zachman have been infused into the Federal Enterprise Architecture Framework (FEAF). DoD has also been creating their own version of the FEA Reference Models to link to the FEAF. The DoDAF products can be easily tied to either of these frameworks. Other frameworks are available, and others will be developed over time. However, frameworks aren't enough; the key to producing a worthwhile, defensible architecture is the underlying methodologies that produce them. If you have a self-consistent methodology that has been proven over time, you should be able to derive products from any framework; it should only be a matter of translating from one notation to another or pulling additional data from your architecture into a similar diagram.

In the next chapters, we will get into the details of our discussion above. As in the preceding discussion, I will provide conclusions derived from my experience. We will end with a summary of where I think the DoDAF is going. Hopefully, you will find a lot of interest in the material in-between. We will attempt to keep it entertaining. Enjoy the ride.

2

What Is DoDAF Anyway?

As we discussed in Chapter 1, there are all kinds of architectures:

◆ House/Building Architecture

◆ Information Architecture

◆ Enterprise Architecture

◆ Technical Architecture

◆ Logical Architecture

◆ Physical Architecture

◆ ...

From all these different "architectures" in differing contexts we might conclude it may be one of the most abused words in the English language today. And we will continue to abuse it throughout this book. But before we add to the list, let's explore what each of the architectures above is about, their characteristics, and where they apply.

The first one, house or building architecture, is clearly the most recognizable by a general audience. This refers to the structure of the building and includes the location of all the electrical plugs, plumbing, and other "interfaces" with the outside world. It adheres to the basic principles of *form, fit, and function*. The *form* is important, as it will provide the style of architecture (modern, classic, etc.) that appeals to the tastes of the owners and architects. The *fit* ensures that the plans meet all the constraints (e.g., size of the lot, building codes, etc.) The *function* of the building is incorporated in the blueprints, as each room will be designated for certain activities (e.g. the kitchen for cooking, the office for work, the bedroom for ... well you get the idea).

The second one, information architecture, refers to the data and resulting information that flows through your organization or system. Information is usually captured in a series of data descriptions, in the form of class diagrams (if you are using object-oriented methods), or entity-relationship-attribute (ERA) diagrams (if you are using structured analysis methods).

The third one, enterprise architecture, refers to the overall architecture of your organization (hence the name enterprise). This "architecture' will include your information, business processes and

11

systems. Another definition for enterprise architectures from the Office of Management and Budget (OMB) is shown in the box below.

The fourth one, technical architecture, is a particularly odd term. It refers to the *standards* that apply to your architecture. What makes this odd is that many people assume this term only applies to

> *"An EA is the explicit description and documentation of the current and desired relationships among business and management processes and information technology."*
>
> OMB Circular A-130

technical standards, such as IPv6 for the Internet. It can (and should) also include operational standards, such as Joint Tactics, Techniques, and Procedures (JTTP) or the Capability Maturity Model-Integrated (CMMI). This type of architecture was done at the DoD level in a document called the Joint Technical Architecture (JTA). This document has been replaced by the DoD Information Technology (IT) Standards Registry (DISR) On-Line. This registry can be accessed on the Defense Information Systems Agency (DISA) websites on SIPRnet and NIPRnet (networks for classified and restricted information).

[handwritten margin note: I believe I have seen this done previously; I should look into it]

The fifth and sixth items on the list, logical and physical architectures, are a more traditional way system engineers have broken out architectures. The logical architecture was represented by the functional flows and data element. The physical architecture was represented by the components of the system and the interfaces between them. To link together the two architectures, you simply allocate functions to components (and data elements to interfaces), hence the terms functional analysis and *allocation*.

As you can see, there are lots of ways to interpret the term "architecture." But you may be asking yourself, "Why should I care?" To determine that we need to discuss how architectures can be useful.

Uses of Architectures by Government and Industry

The answer to that question really begins with the recognition that architecture is being used by commercial, as well as Government, organizations to try to get a better handle on when and what technology they should be investing in. Of course, the driving technology is *information technology (IT)*. The fast pace of IT changes has been and continues to be breath taking. It becomes very hard to predict when the best time is to invest in updating computers, software, servers, networks, and other IT tools. The impact on business processes and training can be prohibitive, in terms of both cost and time, hence the need to control the investment. Architectures help this process by providing insight into the business processes and systems, how they interact with one another and where the technology is being used. By providing traceability between requirements (including those for training, functions, and components), we can determine the impact of changes and determine the best timing for replacements.

In addition to guiding technology investments, the analysis of business processes can often enable you to more effectively conduct your business, thus increasing productivity. This analysis has been called a number of things over time: functional analysis, integrated process design and development, and business process re-engineering, just to name a few. Hence, you can use your architecture to improve the way you do business, with or without changing the underlying technology.

Another use for architectures is to provide a logical means to reorganize your operations. How do companies re-organize today? In reality, most do it around the people. Oh, they may claim it's functional, but how often do they actually look at their business processes and determine which processes can best be grouped together within a particular organization? More often, a company hires someone with a desired, perceived skill set. The, the company, division or office is reorganized around the new personality. If instead, a more objective analysis of the business processes has been performed, you can allocate processes to organizational components (just as you do with functions to systems) and thereby give your organization more coherence and minimize problems between interfacing organizations. You can even trace these functions back to strategic objectives (requirements) and know why a certain organization is necessary for the health of the company (a good way to get rid of deadwood and unnecessary bureaucracy). Can you imaging this approach applied to Government organizations as well? It would give new meaning to Will Rogers' famous statement, "Be thankful we're not getting all the Government we pay for!"[1]

Architectures can also provide a time perspective. In Figure 2-1, we show the different time phases where architectures can be developed.

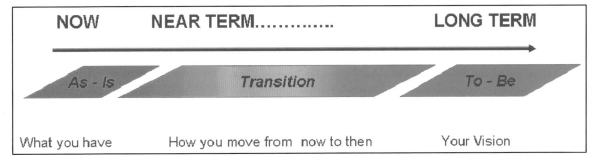

Figure 2-1. Architectures Provide a Means to Deal with the Past, Present and Future.

The "As-Is" architecture represents the elements of your systems and business processes today. Of course that's a moving target, many of these are changing all the time, but it is the best estimate of where they are "today." The "To-Be" architecture depicts where you want to go in terms of new technologies, techniques, and processes. This "To-Be"

---

[1] Obtained from http://www.quotationspage.com, November 2005.

architecture can become the foundation for your long-term strategic plan. The "Transition" architecture provides the means to get from the "As-Is" to the "To-Be." You might define a number of "Transition" architectures, perhaps providing new plans for every five years.

You might ask the questions: "Which is the easiest to do?" and "Which is the hardest to do?" Perhaps the easiest is the "To-Be," since that architecture is the least constrained by technological and political realities of today. However, if you don't have a pretty good crystal ball on- hand, then you might find the "To-Be" very difficult. Some say, the "As-Is" is the easiest, since it exists, and all you are doing is documenting what you have today. However, the "As-Is' is a bit more difficult, because it is a moving target. If the documentation exists, it is usually out of date, and the real processes are hidden in the bureaucracies that form around viable business processes.

The hardest may really be the transitional architectures. These have all the difficulties mentioned above for the "As-Is," but they also have a major problem they must overcome: politics. Why politics? Because the transitional architectures will impact how future money will be spent and hence the budget. Budget development is perhaps the most political thing we do in the Government arena. Everyone is jockeying for position to feed at the trough. Billions are spent on lobbyists, advertising, proposals (both solicited and unsolicited), independent research, and development (IR&D), and overhead, just to obtain future business. This competition is good for the Government since it tends to reduce long-term costs and provide more capability, but it adds to the complexity of producing architectures. Of course, that's why they pay us the big bucks!

As to which ones should you do and in what order, I recommend that you begin with the "As-Is", or at least, portions of it to understand the existing and planned systems/processes. You need to look at these first to identify shortfalls or other related issues, as well as to avoid "reinventing the wheel." By having a firm understanding of what you're doing today, you can then make the "To-Be" (the next step) into a significant improvement, rather than just an incremental one. You need a first cut at the "As-Is" and "To-Be" to develop rational transition architectures. For an example, I watched one architecture effort try to do all three in parallel, with different teams. The transition plan was characterized as a "plan to write a transition plan." Clearly that approach doesn't work well and is frustrating for everyone involved.

Please note that architectures can (and should) be a means of *deriving the necessary requirements*, including system design, test & evaluation (T&E) and operations & support (O&S). Many people see architectures as the production of a number of diagrams that have no real use long term. They treat architecting as an exercise that's been required by management (or in the case of U.S. Federal enterprise architectures – law). If instead we recognize that the correct application of architecture gives us the basic requirements needed to pursue system development and acquisition, we can immediately see the benefits of a well conducted architecture study.

What Is Architecture?

We have discussed different types of architectures and how they might be useful, but we really haven't defined what makes up architectures in detail. So let's look at some definitions for architecture. Let's start with the one from the DoDAF itself. The definition[2] is provided in the box on the right. Whereas this definition gives a good short definition, it doesn't really tell us what information we need to gather to describe the architecture. However, DoDAF goes well beyond this simple definition. It breaks architecture into three views (actually four, but who's counting): operational, systems and technical standards. Figure 2-2 provides a depiction[3] of the three views.

> **Architecture:** the structure of components, their relationships, and the principles and guidelines governing their design and evolution over time.
> *DoD Integrated Architecture Panel, 1995*

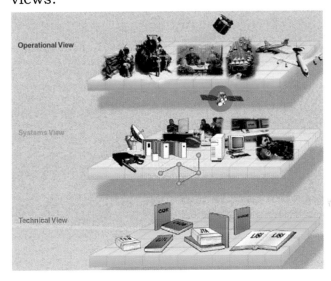

Figure 2-2. DoDAF Views: What's missing?

This drawing has some interesting implications. First, notice that the different views lie on different, unconnected planes. One might infer that they are independent of one another. This thought comes from this idea that you can treat these as separate "architectures" by themselves, which goes back to C4ISR Architecture Framework, Version 1.0, as discussed in Chapter 1. Another "missing item" is the lack of any attempt to depict the business processes – no flow diagrams or process/procedure books. It seems it's all about the hardware and software (with maybe a little people thrown in). Another "problem" with this diagram is the possible implication that technical standards are static. *I often think they should have cobwebs on the books.* However, those of us involved in the world of IT standards know how rapidly they are changing. New web standards are coming out

---

[2] DoD Architecture Framework 1.0, 9 February 2004, Volume I, p. 1-1

[3] From the "Integrated DoD Architectures" brochure, available at http://www.dod.mil/c3i/org/cio/i3/AWG_Digital_Library/pdfdocs/brochure.pdf

all the time. With the advent of Service-Oriented Architectures (SOA), we can envision even more changes just down the road.

But enough of beating up on the DoDAF definition, let's see what other definitions we can find for architectures. Melissa Cook in her book entitled *Building Enterprise Information Architectures*, doesn't have a definition, but says: "An architecture provides the basis for business control over the contractors.[4]" Whereas, we know that contractors are basically uncontrollable, without an architecture you don't stand a chance. This book is a must read for those who are trying wrestle with creating an Enterprise Architecture or an Information Architecture.

Another popular architecture book is the one by Maier and Rechtin, *The Art of Systems Architecting*. In it, architecture is defined as "The structure (in terms of components, connections, and constraints) of a product, process, or element.[5]" This definition begins to define the parameters that are needed to describe an architecture (components, connections and constraints). It also provides a number of "rules of thumb" for developing good architectures; architecture isn't just an engineering discipline – it is also an art form.

A third book provides another perspective on decomposition by views. Dennis Buede's seminal system engineering text includes the following: *"Levis [1993] has defined an analytical systems engineering process that ... includes three separate architectures (functional, physical, and operational) ...[6]"* Dennis' book is currently used in many schools of system engineering as a basic textbook.

By looking at all of these definitions and thinking more about the parameters that can be used to describe architectures, we may have developed a more useful definition (see box on right).

This definition implies that we need many parameters (or dimensions) to completely describe the architecture, including risks, decisions, data, systems, components, organizations, functions, requirements, performance, etc. Although this is potentially a substantial list (around 20 parameters or so), it is finite and can be gathered in a reasonable amount of time. Notice that I have included parameters that you might consider as "programmatic, such as risks and decisions. Also, I have included those parameters because we see architecture development in a similar light as system engineering: they

> **Architecture:** *A fundamental and unifying structure defined in terms of elements, information, interfaces, processes, constraints, and behaviors.*

---

[4] Building Enterprise Information Architectures, Melissa A. Cook, 1996, p. 13, Prentice Hall PTR.

[5] The Art of Systems Architecting, Mark W. Maier and Eberhardt Rechtin, 2002, p. 285, CRC Press, Inc.

[6] The Engineering Design of Systems, Dennis M. Buede, 2000, p. 19, John Wiley & Sons, Inc.

both have technical and management aspects.

You may also note that we have explicitly included "behaviors" in our definition. "Why is behavior important (and what is it)?" Behavior refers to the way an architecture works, usually expressed in terms of the functions performed, resource used, and overall systems performance. As architects, we want to control the behavior of the systems captured in the architecture, not have "emergent" or unpredictable behavior. For a warfighter, even good, but unexpected behaviors might get them killed. Hence, we take the "Holiday Inn" approach (*the best surprise is no surprise[7]*).

Well, now that we have a working definition for architectures, we need to explore the adjective "executable" as applied to architecture. *Executable architecture* refers to the use of dynamic simulation software to evaluate architecture models. What do executable architectures do for us? They:

♦ verify the logic of operational activities and system functions;

♦ estimate timing concerns;

♦ estimate impact on resources; and

♦ analyze architecture measures, including cost-benefit tradeoffs.

The bottom line is: we need to be sure our architectures work before going to the system design level. By developing an executable architecture, we can verify that the logic is correct and that it has predictable performance. Very few of the architecture developments to date within the DoD (and the rest of the Government and industry for that matter) are truly executable. Often we don't discover the problems until much further down stream in the development process and thus end up incurring much greater costs to fix the problems we do find.

What Is the DoD Architecture Framework?

The next question in your mind must be "so what's this framework?" "Is it an architecture or what?" To answer this, we need to recognize that the DoDAF was developed as a means to compare architectures. It is not an architecture or a methodology to develop architectures. Instead, it enables this comparison by defining a set of views of an architecture (a.k.a. products). These products were grouped into 4 views:

♦ Operational View;

♦ Technical Standards View;

♦ Systems View; and

♦ All-View

---

[7] "The Best Surprise is No Surprise" is a trademark of Holiday Inn, Inc.

The all-view products are meant to cut across and link the other three views, but these are just views of your architecture. As we discussed in Chapter 1, the three categories of views (operational, systems and technical) are just a way to divide up the architecture so that different constituents can have the views they find most useful and interesting. In fact, you may think about the way we currently break up DoD into Commands, Services and Agencies (CSA). Commands perform the warfighting or "operational" tasks. Services [Army, Navy, Air Force] provide the equipment and training (i.e. "systems") to conduct operations. Agencies (of the Office of the Secretary of Defense) provide "standards" for conducting the warfighting (and contribute to the acquisition process). Hence, the idea to divide up architecture in these three categories may have been affected by the political decomposition we use every day.

Is this a bad thing? No, we should always want to portray the architecture in ways that best communicate the results to different groups of users. The fact that we have the CSA structure in DoD is a good thing. Also, it is intelligent to formulate a means of architecture comparison that follows along those lines. However, as you can imagine it can be a disaster in trying to develop architectures, because the *three views overlap*. In watching people try to "wire together" the products, they miss this point. A number of methodologies have been developed that make this attempt. As a practitioner and observer of architecture development, I have found that trying to use the Framework as a basis for methodology leads to very poor, non-executable architectures. In Chapter 5, we will discuss "good" methodologies for developing architectures.

But first, let's try to understand more about the DoDAF itself. First of all, the DoDAF products are represented in many different forms: graphics, text, and tables (see Figure 2-3). The DoDAF specifies the information content for products in each view, but not the specific form (see quote in box above). Many people look at the diagrams associated with the DoDAF (and the document calls many of them "templates"), but you should have the flexibility and freedom to present the information in the most useful way to the people who are using or evaluating the architecture. However, many people interpret the diagrams as the mandatory formats and representations for DoDAF compliance.

The specific products developed depend on the intended use of the architecture, as we will see later in this chapter.

> "The Framework does not advocate the use of any one methodology (e.g., structured analysis vs. object orientation), or one notation over another (IDEF1X or ER notation) to complete this step, but products should contain the required information and relationships."
>
> DoD Architecture Framework, Version 1.0 (09 February 2004) Vol. II, p. 2-8

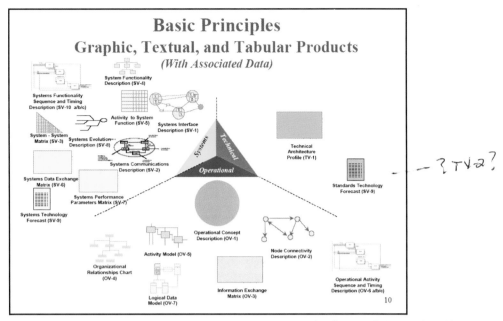

Figure 2-3. Presented by Mr. Truman Parmele at the DoD Architectures Conference February 24, 2004.

Additional products are allowed if they improve communication of the architecture. In fact, most people will tell you that the set of products is insufficient to provide the views needed by everyone. As you can see, this need for additional "products" or views implies the need for a more complete approach to architecture development. Development of additional worthwhile products requires a well-founded, well-applied methodology based on the rigorous application of systems engineering principles. *In fact, the original intent of the DoDAF was to encourage the use of system engineering methodologies to develop architectures.*

The next step in gaining a better understanding of the DoDAF comes from knowing some of the key concepts and definition associated with it. As we discuss these, we will also identify and discuss several myths that surround the Architecture Framework.

2.1 What Are the Key DoDAF Concepts and Definitions?

Let's start with a brief discussion of the Framework's philosophy. As we have previously stated, the DoDAF provides guidance for describing architectures. It is *not* a "How To" build architectures document. The DoDAF provides the rules, guidance, and product descriptions.

The DoDAF provides some, but not all, of the parameters that enable comparison. For example, one of the products deals with performance, but no metrics are provided. None of the products explicitly deal with cost (clearly an important parameter for decision makers).

The DoDAF now provides guidance to the entire Department. No longer can organizations outside the C4ISR domain ignore this guidance. As we will see in the next chapter, DoDAF products are required in virtually all the major DoD acquisition policies. The budget for your

JCIDS-NR KPP- Mandatory DoDAF products

program now depends on having DoDAF products available for evaluation by the Joint Staff and OSD.

Perhaps one of the most important philosophical comments about the DoDAF comes from the box on the right. This quote recognizes that the United States doesn't fight wars alone. In every major conflict, throughout the history of our nation we have had allies who we must work with to win. For those who don't think so, imagine where this nation would have been with out the French Navy during the Revolutionary War.

> *"... defines a common approach for Department of Defense (DoD) architecture description development, presentation, and integration. The Framework is intended to ensure that architecture descriptions can be compared and related across organizational boundaries, including Joint and multinational boundaries."*
>
> *DoD Architecture Framework, Version 1.0 (09 February 2004) Volume II, p.1-1*

The fact that DoD has now defined these architecture views also means that those organizations within and without the U.S. who we work with have a great interest in the DoDAF. England has the "MODAF" (Ministry of Defence Architecture Framework). Australia has their "DAF" (Defence Architecture Framework). These other frameworks are modeled after the DoDAF and also, extend the views. For example, the DAF defines Common (CV) and Data (DV) Views in addition to the operational, systems and technical.

All this philosophical discussion leads us to our first "myth."

Myth #1: The Framework provides a definitive means for comparing architectures

♦ *In reality, the Framework and in particular the essential products do not provide enough information for decision makers*

  o *No common metrics are provided for comparing performance or cost*

  o *The architectures could actually reference different levels of decomposition, no hierarchy was defined*

♦ *These limitations were noted at the time and were determined to be too difficult to arrive at that time. The assumption at the time was that version 3.0 would try to resolve these deficiencies*

As those who know the differences between the C4ISR Architecture Framework 2.0 and DoDAF 1.0 can readily attest, Version 3.0 hasn't arrived yet. The improvements in the DoDAF still don't address these fundamental issues. However, some progress along these lines is underway in the DoDAF 2.0 work.

Now that we understand some of the underlying philosophy, let's look at some of the concepts, some of which may be new to you (as they were to me) that were put forth by the Framework.

Framework Concepts

We have discussed the architecture views: Operational, Systems, Technical Standards, All-Views, and the linkage among the views being highly dependent upon each other. In addition to these concepts, we need to understand what the DoDAF means by architecture measures, net-centricity, and the application of the new warfighting paradigm: TPPU.

The DoDAF defines a hierarchy of architecture measures:

◆ Mission Measures of Effectiveness, which are generally subjective;

◆ Capability Needs, which are measurable; and

◆ System Measures of Performance, which provide specification-level measures.

Figure 2-4 shows how these measures relate to the overall architecture development process.[8] These seems a bit odd, in that a mission measure of effectiveness is considered subjective (how can something measurable be subjective?), yet a capability need is considered measurable. But these are their definitions and we need to understand and use them if we are going to effectively communicate.

Figure 2-4. Cross-View Linkages and Measurements.

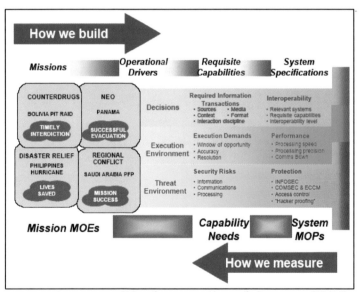

Unfortunately, when this hierarchy was developed, the authors must have been unaware of a similar decompos-ition used by the test and evaluation community (T&E). They define a similar hierarchy of measurements as: critical operational issues (COI), measures of effectiveness (MOE), and measures of performance (MOP). The definition of these terms is similar to the ones used for Mission MOEs, Capability Needs, and System MOPs. I mention this distinction only to help avoid confusion. When architects talk to people in the T&E business – as they should since Operational Test and Evaluation (OT&E) represent the way architectures are validated by the warfighter – they need to know this distinction.

Net-Centricity has been all the rage in DoD. Net centricity means the use of internet-like networks (those using Internet Protocols, such as NIPRnet, SIPRnet, and JWICS) to make information and applications available to whoever needs it, whenever they need it. Major new

---

[8] DoD Architecture Framework v. 1.0, 9 February 2004, Volume I, p. 4-5

architectures are using net-centric concepts, including Future Combat Systems (FCS) for the Army and Net Centric Enterprise Services (NCES) at Defense Information Systems Agency (DISA). Net centricity requires reliable, fast access to the network to accomplish these tasks. When net-centric operations and warfare (NCOW) was proposed in the mid-1990's by the Navy, the internet boom was in full force. We anticipated, due to the number of satellite (low earth orbit) and terrestrial networks in development, that we would have access to 10 Megabits/second at low latencies. Unfortunately, most of those network developments collapsed with the "dot com" bust of 2000. The lack of the availability of *ubiquitous* communications means that our architectures have had to deal with the high bandwidth and low bandwidth users, making full net-centricity problematic for the warfighter. The concept of enclaves (capabilities pushed to the low bandwidth user) has recently gained interest and acceptance in the DoD community.

Net-centricity also leads to another concept we want to discuss, TPPU: Task, Post, Process, and Use. TPPU replaces TPED (Task, Process, Exploit, and Disseminate), which has been the concept in the Agencies, Services, and Intelligence Community for decades. TPED implies that the information gathered by various (usually highly classified) sensor systems, would not be available until dissemination. This process implies significant amounts of time were necessary, since the "raw" sensor data had to be processed on the ground and even then it was difficult for anyone except an intelligence analyst to decipher and put into context.

However, with modern sensor systems many of which can be operated at lower levels of classification, such as the streaming video from the Predator, warfighters can obtain immediate access to time critical information. Figure 2-5 represents a typical TPPU scenario.

Step 1 (Task) represents the process of tasking an information gather asset (in this case a Predator that then discovers an enemy missile launcher).

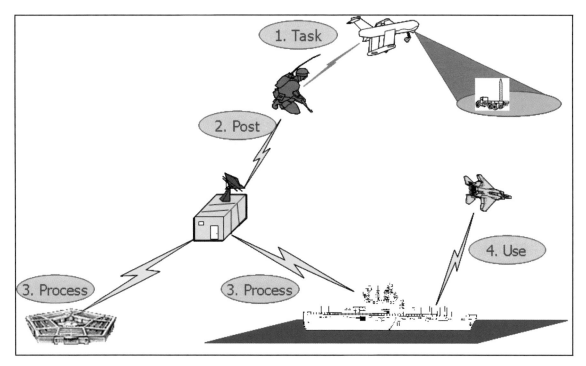

Figure 2-5. TPPU – Task, Post, Process, and Use.

Step 2 (Post) means the unanalyzed collected information is made available to any authorized user. Step 3 (Process) means that multiple users can process the information to enable them to make a variety of strategic (e.g. Pentagon), operational, or tactical (task a strike aircraft) decisions. Step 4 (Use) shows how the information can be used, in this case a strike aircraft receives ad hoc tasking to destroy the missile launcher.

Now that we understand some of the underlying concepts, let's look at some of the key definitions.

Framework Definitions

Let's start with the views. An **Operational View** is defined as "... description of the tasks and activities, operational elements, and information exchanges required to accomplish DoD missions.[9]" Notice that this definition includes functional things (tasks and activities), as well as physical (operational elements). The people can be represented as "operational elements" although this is often assumed to be organizations. We can however represent individual people or roles in the operation.

The **Systems View** is defined as "... description ... of systems and interconnections providing for, or supporting, DoD functions.[10]" This

COMMANDS

---

[9] DoD Architecture Framework v. 1.0, 9 February 2004, Volume I, p. 1-2

[10] DoD Architecture Framework v. 1.0, 9 February 2004, Volume I, p. 1-2

definition implies only hardware and software (systems and interconnections), but when we look further we find system functions and the operators of the hardware and software (at least). Hence, as we have said before, the operational and systems views both have logical and physical aspects to them.

The **Technical Standards View** is defined as "... minimal set of rules governing the arrangement, interaction, and interdependence of system parts or elements ...[11]" The implication from this definition is that standards only apply to systems or at least the systems view. We should capture operational standards as part of the architecture as we stated before and will continue to state again and again. The focus on systems-related standards may be due to the interest in interoperability and the misconception that interoperability is mostly a systems problem. As most communications experts will tell you, for complete communications to occur, it requires standards at all levels, including the language and context. Language depends on the standardization of terms and context often includes assumptions on the processes being accomplished, and so, technical standards should include operational standards (those that tie to the operational views) as well.

The definition of **All Views** includes the "... overarching aspects of an architecture that relate to all three of the views.[12]" By the inclusion of this view, we can see that the three other views do not stand alone. Information presented in the all view products link and constrains the three views together.

Some other interesting (and maybe unfamiliar) terms are nodes, IERs, and needlines. These three terms come from the communications domain. Nodes represent "an element of architecture that produces, consumes, or processes data.[13]" I find this definition interesting since now that the Framework applies DoD-wide, we might be interested in more than just data. For example, we might want to define "nodes" that produce, consume, or process bullets, replacement parts, and even meals ready to eat (MREs). Please note, it is possible to have both operational and system nodes. They can represent the same things (such as organizational units), or they can be different (organization vs. facility).

Information Exchange Requirements (IERs) are defined as: "A requirement for information that is exchanged between nodes.[14]" The requirement includes performance attributes such as size, throughput, timeliness, quality, and quantity values. This concept appears to combine the data with the "pipes" it flows through. In system

---

[11] DoD Architecture Framework v. 1.0, 9 February 2004, Volume I, p. 1-3

[12] DoD Architecture Framework v. 1.0, 9 February 2004, Volume I, p. 1-3

[13] DoD Architecture Framework v. 1.0, 9 February 2004, Volume II, p. B-4

[14] DoD Architecture Framework v. 1.0, 9 February 2004, Volume II, p. B-2

engineering practice, we usually separate these two concepts, since data belongs to the logical architecture, and the physical "pipes" (often called links or interfaces) provide constraints usually captured in the physical architecture. This SE approach enables us to easily "upgrade" the physical architecture without changing the logical architecture (think technology insertion). If we combine the two concepts it makes dealing with physical component changes and therefore interfaces much more difficult, *thus potentially making interoperability more problematic.*

The last of these communications-based terms is needlines. Needlines are defined as "A requirement that is the logical expression of the need to transfer information among nodes.[15]" Again in system engineering parlance this means a logical interface between two nodes. We see needlines and IERs only in reference to the operational views. The equivalent on the system view side is interfaces and data. Again, these definitions tend to limit the characterization to an IT domain problem, which we must broaden to be successful in applying these terms DoD-wide.

The next term of interest is capabilities. The Joint Capability Integration and Development System (JCIDS) policy defines capability as "the ability to execute a specified course of action. It is defined by an operational user and expressed in broad operational terms in the format of an initial capabilities document or a DOTMLPF change recommendation.[16]" The DoDAF provides the following example: "A capability may be defined in terms of the attributes required to accomplish a set of activities ... in order to achieve a given mission objective.[17]" Figure 2-6[18] shows the relationship between capabilities and the mission, threads and operational activities, according to the Framework.

This diagram shows that capabilities provide a way to organize the missions/courses of action described in the concept of operations (CONOPS). In turn, we can define capabilities as one or more operational threads, which consist of operational activities (see definition below). With a diagram like this you are probably asking "where do I start?" If you are working "top down" you want to define the basic mission that the architecture should perform. From that information, you can identify the capabilities needed, but that may be difficult to do in advance of some analysis. We have found that defining various scenarios (or threads as they are called above) is an easier place to start. You can analyze the threads by identifying the activities and create process models or behavior diagrams (which will be described in detail in Chapter 5) to

---

[15] DoD Architecture Framework v. 1.0, 9 February 2004, Volume II, p. B-3

[16] CJCSI 3170.01D, 12 March 2004, p. GL-4

[17] DoD Architecture Framework v. 1.0, 9 February 2004, Volume II, p. 4-37

[18] DoD Architecture Framework v. 1.0, 9 February 2004, Deskbook, p. 3-3

determine the viability of the scenarios. Also note that a collection of scenarios usually forms the basis for the CONOPS, hence, this circular process is correct in that you need to iterate through these steps several times to have a well described capabilities-based architecture.

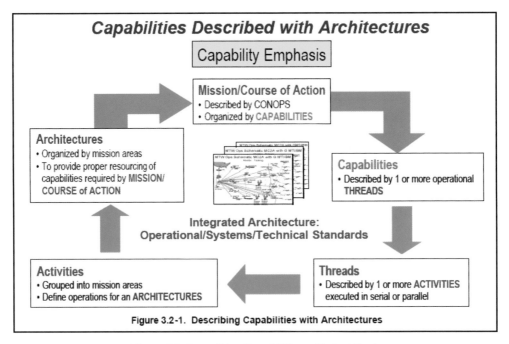

Figure 3.2-1. Describing Capabilities with Architectures

Figure 2-6. Describing Capabilities with Architectures.

The last definitions we want to discuss here are the ones for operational activities and system functions. We will deal with them together for what we hope will become obvious reasons.

The Framework defines an operational activity as: "an action performed in conducting the business of an enterprise. It is a general term that does not imply a placement in a hierarchy (e.g., it could be a process or a task as defined in other documents and it could be at any level of the hierarchy of the Operational Activity Model). It is used to portray operational actions not hardware/software system functions."[19] The Framework defines system function as a "data transform that supports the automation of activities or information elements exchange."[20] In another part of the Framework, we find the following caveat: "System functions are not limited to internal system functions and can include Human Computer Interface (HCI) and Graphical User Interface (GUI) functions or functions."[21]

Many architects have interpreted these definitions to mean that operational activities are what people do and system functions are all

---

[19] DoD Architecture Framework v. 1.0, 9 February 2004, Volume I, p. B-4

[20] DoD Architecture Framework v. 1.0, 9 February 2004, Volume I, p. B-5

[21] DoD Architecture Framework v. 1.0, 9 February 2004, Volume II, p. 5-25

26

about the hardware and software. In fact, as we will see in the next section, the DoDAF products that describe the operational activities and system functions require the same types of information (decomposition, inputs, outputs, time, and sequencing). Hence, they are really describing similar things. These two categories of information, therefore, represent what system engineers classically referred to as the results of functional analysis and *allocation*. We emphasize allocation, because assigning these functions (and now we've generally classed operational activities and systems functions into the general classification of "functions" i.e. the transformation of inputs into outputs) to people or things is simply the process of identifying how the functions are implemented.

Other architects prefer to see operational activities as the higher level abstraction of the system functions. So they decompose operational activities into system functions and then allocate them to people or things, as appropriate for implementation.

Neither approach is right or wrong. Both approaches can help to better understand the problems you want to solve. You just need to be consistent in the application of the approach.

Now that we have some of the definitions used by the Framework, let's see what the products contain. We will just provide an overview and some insights into the product sets for details on each of these products see the referenced sections of the DoDAF volumes.

2.2. What Are the DoDAF Products?

The DoDAF products are summarized in Figure 2-7.[22] As you can see, the groupings of products fall into the four categories of views discussed above. The first set of views, the "All Views" or common views, consist of only two products: the AV-1 which provides an "executive summary" of the architecture and the AV-2, which represents the complete set of architecture "definitions." Please note that this is not simply a glossary (please see Section 2.2.3 for a fuller discussion as to why).

The next set is the operational views. The OVs include a high level concept diagram (OV-1 or the "cartoon" as we like to call it), interface diagrams, OV-2 & OV3), organizational chart (OV-4), functional analysis products (OV-5 & 6), and the logical data model (OV-7).

---

[22] DoD Architecture Framework v. 1.0, 9 February 2004, Volume I, p. 1-4

Table 1-1. Architecture Products

Applicable View	Framework Product	Framework Product Name	General Description
All Views	AV-1	Overview and Summary Information	Scope, purpose, intended users, environment depicted, analytical findings
All Views	AV-2	Integrated Dictionary	Architecture data repository with definitions of all terms used in all products
Operational	OV-1	High-Level Operational Concept Graphic	High-level graphical/textual description of operational concept
Operational	OV-2	Operational Node Connectivity Description	Operational nodes, connectivity, and information exchange needlines between nodes
Operational	OV-3	Operational Information Exchange Matrix	Information exchanged between nodes and the relevant attributes of that exchange
Operational	OV-4	Organizational Relationships Chart	Organizational, role, or other relationships among organizations
Operational	OV-5	Operational Activity Model	Capabilities, operational activities, relationships among activities, inputs, and outputs; overlays can show cost, performing nodes, or other pertinent information
Operational	OV-6a	Operational Rules Model	One of three products used to describe operational activity—identifies business rules that constrain operation
Operational	OV-6b	Operational State Transition Description	One of three products used to describe operational activity—identifies business process responses to events
Operational	OV-6c	Operational Event-Trace Description	One of three products used to describe operational activity—traces actions in a scenario or sequence of events
Operational	OV-7	Logical Data Model	Documentation of the system data requirements and structural business process rules of the Operational View
Systems	SV-1	Systems Interface Description	Identification of systems nodes, systems, and system items and their interconnections, within and between nodes
Systems	SV-2	Systems Communications Description	Systems nodes, systems, and system items, and their related communications lay-downs
Systems	SV-3	Systems-Systems Matrix	Relationships among systems in a given architecture; can be designed to show relationships of interest, e.g., system-type interfaces, planned vs. existing interfaces, etc.
Systems	SV-4	Systems Functionality Description	Functions performed by systems and the system data flows among system functions
Systems	SV-5	Operational Activity to Systems Function Traceability Matrix	Mapping of systems back to capabilities or of system functions back to operational activities
Systems	SV-6	Systems Data Exchange Matrix	Provides details of system data elements being exchanged between systems and the attributes of that exchange
Systems	SV-7	Systems Performance Parameters Matrix	Performance characteristics of Systems View elements for the appropriate time frame(s)
Systems	SV-8	Systems Evolution Description	Planned incremental steps toward migrating a suite of systems to a more efficient suite, or toward evolving a current system to a future implementation
Systems	SV-9	Systems Technology Forecast	Emerging technologies and software/hardware products that are expected to be available in a given set of time frames and that will affect future development of the architecture
Systems	SV-10a	Systems Rules Model	One of three products used to describe system functionality—identifies constraints that are imposed on systems functionality due to some aspect of systems design or implementation
Systems	SV-10b	Systems State Transition Description	One of three products used to describe system functionality—identifies responses of a system to events
Systems	SV-10c	Systems Event-Trace Description	One of three products used to describe system functionality—identifies system-specific refinements of critical sequences of events described in the Operational View
Systems	SV-11	Physical Schema	Physical implementation of the Logical Data Model entities, e.g., message formats, file structures, physical schema
Technical	TV-1	Technical Standards Profile	Listing of standards that apply to Systems View elements in a given architecture
Technical	TV-2	Technical Standards Forecast	Description of emerging standards and potential impact on current Systems View elements, within a set of time frames

Figure 2-7. Summary of the DoDAF Products.

The third set consists of the system views. The SVs include several different versions of interface diagrams (SV-1, SV-2, SV-3, and SV-6), functional analysis products (SV-4, SV-5, SV-10), a performance matrix (SV-7), transition planning diagrams (SV-8, SV-9), and finally the physical data model (SV-11).

The last set is the technical views. The TVs only have two standards views: the first of the current (or near term projected) standards and the second a forecast of the standards that may come into play over the life of the architecture.

Most of these products are classical system engineering products, in particular the interface, functional analysis, and data models. In fact, they are a subset of the total products we might expect from a complete system engineering analysis. They were chosen to represent the primary kinds of products a decision maker might need to make investment decisions. But how do we know what ones are needed? The next section discusses this.

2.2.1 How Should We Select the Products?

In the predecessor to the DoDAF (C4ISR Architecture Framework 2.0) products were separated into "essential" and "supporting." The essential products (AV-1, AV-2, OV-1, OV-2, OV-3, SV-1, and TV-1) were determined necessary for all architecture studies. This minimum set would be expanded as needed and when more detailed analyses were desired. Towards the end of the panel discussion on the products, Figure 2-8[23] was produced and adopted as a good way of visualizing the application of products for the development of succeeding levels of detail.

Although this diagram was a "conceptual relationship" and not a hard and fast rule, many people began to treat this diagram as a "cookie cutter," thus when we received an RFP for a system design the Government required that we produce all the products (whether they made any sense or not … and it didn't), as this diagram suggests.

In the DoDAF, the idea of essential and supporting was removed. Instead a table "to provide initial insights into the use of various products"[24] was provided, as reproduced in Figure 2-9.[25] This table gives an architect a starting point for determining the necessary products for a specific type of architecture analysis. Note that while it's a good starting point, it can't be used as a "cookie cutter" for all situations. For example, take business process reengineering (BPR – the last row in Figure 2-9. One of the driving forces behind a BPR analysis is changing technology. Often, processes are developed with and older technology, such as databases and spreadsheets for managing customer relationships. A new technology comes along which integrates information from various databases into a single, coherent Customer Relationship Manager (CRM) package. That new technology will require new business processes to be implemented, hence the obvious need for operational views. But the software package, the hardware it must run

---

[23] C4ISR Architecture Framework, Version 2.0 December 18, 1997, p. 4-2

[24] DoD Architecture Framework v. 1.0, 9 February 2004, Volume I, p. 3-10

[25] DoD Architecture Framework v. 1.0, 9 February 2004, Volume I, p. 3-12

on, other interfacing software, networks and perhaps the entire IT infrastructure, may be affected by bringing this new capability into the operational environment. Hence, we may want SV and TV products to show the impact.

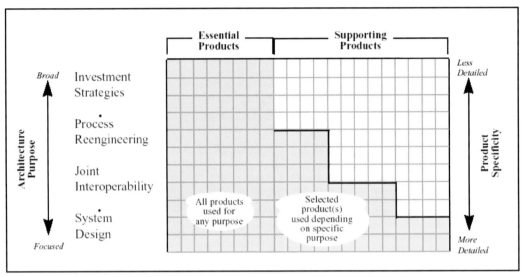

Figure 2-8. An early approach to product selection.

Figure 2-9. DoDAF 1.0's approach to product selection.

Similarly, the table indicates that the OV-1 (the cartoon) isn't needed for Portfolio Management, System Design and Development, and Integrated Test & Evaluation. Actually, it's hard not to have this diagram for all projects, since it is likely the best communications tool you will have or at least the one most everyone will feel comfortable reading.

Clearly this table doesn't preclude the architect from choosing other products to help communicate the results of the analyses, but beware that many customers will wonder why you don't just do what Figure 2-9 says. So be prepared to justify the development of additional products or removing them from the list. You may even decide that the products available in the DoDAF are insufficient (which is usually the case) and that you need to create other products not provided within the Framework. Nothing precludes you from doing this ... expect perhaps your customer. Work with your customer and any evaluators to obtain an agreement on which products get produced and which ones don't.

How Can We Tailor the Products?

The Framework doesn't provide a simple set of tailoring guidelines, as many of the old Military Standards (MIL-STD) did. So we have to think about what makes sense, rather than apply some formula developed by the writers of the DoDAF. First we recommend using the guidance given in the previous section (Figure 2-9) as a starting point. Using the discussion above will help you in determining which of the DoDAF products make the most sense for communicating the results of your architecture development.

Then we need to recognize that the DoDAF products were originally chosen for C4ISR system, not enterprise architectures. So, you may want to look at other frameworks, such as Zachman or the Federal Enterprise Architecture Framework, to identify other products. Other countries have also recognized the shortfall in the DoDAF products and have created their own. Canada has developed their "IDEA Framework," which includes a decision support framework, a transformation Framework and the DND Architecture Framework. The DND (Department of National Defense) Framework is an extension of the DoDAF. They have added products with in the OVs and TVs and expanded the views to include *information views* and *security views*. The British and Australians have developed similar frameworks and a NATO Framework is also under development.

Another factor for tailoring you may want to consider is the timeframe of the architecture. If you are working on the "as-is" architecture, the primary goal is to understand the underlying functional requirements of the current systems, so you can identify shortfalls and places where new technologies and processes can enhance you capabilities. Hence, you may not want to spend too much time creating system hardware/software view products, as these might be changing significantly. Perhaps identifying the key interfaces and creating the SV-6 for those interfaces only may be enough. However, you probably want to spend a significant amount of time analyzing the functional aspects, thus the OV-5/OV6 and SV-4/SV-10 products may be of great interest to decision makers who want to understand the detailed processes.

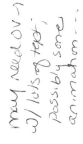

If you are developing a 'to-be" architecture, the future systems may be nebulous, so spending a lot of time developing SVs again may be less desirable. However, concept diagrams would be a great interest and you may decide that the OV-1 is insufficient for this. Artist conceptions of future systems are very helpful in communicating a vision that people can grasp. Again, we recommend spending most of the effort on functional analysis products, as they will be useful regardless of how the systems themselves evolve.

If you're working on a near-term transitional architecture, you will need to understand the details of the systems that are affected by the architecture. Clearly the SV-8 and SV-9 products play an important role, but so will the SV-1/2, SV-6, and SV-7. A heavy emphasis on the resulting system performance (current and future) should be of interest to any decision maker, as will schedule and cost. Although schedule is somewhat handled in the SV-8, cost has no view in the current DoDAF, except as an "overlay" on existing diagrams. Clearly you will need to communicate cost, schedule, and performance of any architecture. (We discuss this more in Chapter 7.)

As you can see, this isn't easy. It will require a significant amount of effort and communication with your customer (and perhaps you customer's customer) to effectively portray the results of you architecture work. Try to do this "up front" or at least early in the program, otherwise, you may not gather all the information your customer needs to make the best decisions.

Tailoring, of course isn't the only concern. You need to understand how the products are linked together to have an integrated architecture that can be traversed quickly and easily to answer the questions that concern decision makers. The next section discusses the linkages (and lack there of) between the current DoDAF products. From this discussion you will see why you need a coherent methodology that fills the gaps in the DoDAF.

2.2.2 How Are the DoDAF Products Related to One Another?

First, you need to realize that the DoDAF products were originally selected as a set of paper "views" that would represent the results of an architecture study. So they were not designed as a coherent set of views that are tightly coupled. As the DoDAF and CADM have evolved, a significant amount of work has been expended to create an integrated architecture model, but it still suffers from this initial approach of independently selected products.

To better understand this, let's look at how the DoDAF visualizes the linkages between the views and diagrams. Figure 2-10 reproduces the very first diagrams, on the very first page of the very first volume of the DoDAF.[26] The diagram shows three views (operational, systems, and technical standards) and how they must be linked together. What's interesting in this diagram is that it is missing the 4th view: All Views. The All Views (AVs) form the underlying linkages between the other views. In particular, the AV-2 contains the "metadata" for the views, and hence any linkages between elements of the architecture. The AV-2 doesn't specify all the necessary linkages (or relationships), only the ones in the CADM. You may be using another database structure that goes beyond the CADM or have extended the CADM to meet the particular needs of your architecture study.

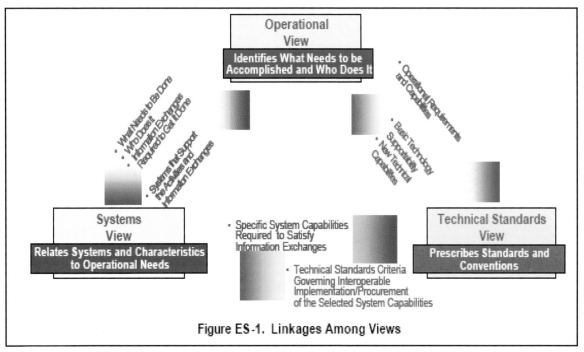

Figure ES-1. Linkages Among Views

Figure 2-10. High Level depiction of the linkages between 3 of the 4 views.

Note the linkage between the operational view and the technical standards view. This diagram shows that the technical standards will be impacted by the operational requirements and capabilities, while the operational view will be affected by basic technology supportability and new technical capabilities. This means that we should have explicit linkages between the TVs and the OVs. However, as Figure 2-12[27] shows, those linkages do not appear in the product level linkage charts and in fact do not appear directly in the TV products themselves.

The DoDAF assumes that all technical standards reference systems, not operational elements. It seems to forget about the operational

---

[26] DoD Architecture Framework v. 1.0, 9 February 2004, Volume I, p. ES-1

[27] DoD Architecture Framework v. 1.0, 9 February 2004, Volume I, p. 3-5

All right — I guess that I do need to read this puppy

Shortcoming just

standards, such as Joint Tactics, Techniques and Procedures, the Universal Joint Task List (UJTL), and Capability Maturity Model Integrated (CMMI). These and many other operational standards are not included in the TV products. We recommend adding linkages between the operational elements and the standards.

Another problem area is the linkage internal to the views, particularly between the OV-5/OV-6 and SV-4/SV-10. These views constitute the "processes" (data flow and functional sequencing) that capture the essence of the architecture's capabilities. Please note, the OV-6 and most of the SVs do not show up in Figure 2-11. Although the CADM shows linkages between these products (because they have overlapping data elements), many times the actual linkages are not developed as these products are generated separately (and even independently).

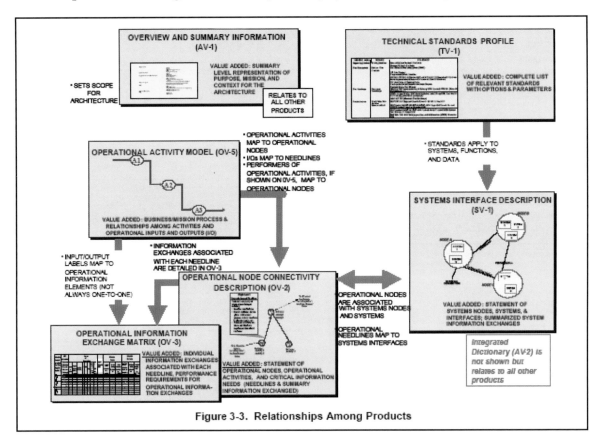

Figure 3-3. Relationships Among Products

Figure 2-11. Not a tightly coupled set of linkages between the products themselves.

In summary, the linkages are mostly within the CADM, but as most architects are not using a CADM-based tool or some other tightly coupled technique, they are dependent on providing the linkages themselves. Having the linkages buried in the CADM or not explicit so that the architect can access them quickly makes tracking down answers to questions very difficult. Imagine what would happen when you are briefing a senior decision maker and she asks you how you got your finding. If you can't come up with an answer quickly, your entire effort will be suspected. Avoid this by ensuring that however you build your architecture, the linkages between the products are explicit and complete.

In the remainder of this chapter, I will summarize the DoDAF products providing some specific insights into the development of these products that will help you better understand and employ them. I do not mean these sections are meant to replace the DoDAF, only supplement it. Please read the product descriptions in the DoDAF carefully, particularly Volume II. They provide details you will need to create a DoDAF-compliant architecture.

2.2.3 What Are the All View (AV) Products?

As we saw in Figure 2-7, there are only two AV products: the AV-1 (Overview and Summary Information) and the AV-2 (Integrated Dictionary). Let's look at each of these in turn.

AV-1 – The Executive Summary of Your Architecture

We often call the AV-1 the "executive summary" of the architecture. The purpose of this document is to capture the driving forces behind the architecture and its results (called findings). Figure 2-12 shows a "representative format"[28] for the AV-1.

The first portion of it contains information that you should know very early in you study. In fact, we recommend that you complete all the AV-1 sections below, except for the finding as early as possible. You might even want to deliver it as a draft to your customers to ensure that you and they are in synch at the very start of the project. This first portion can be short – a few pages are all that are necessary. Figure 2-13 shows an example of this product from the Framework.[29] As you can see many of the entries are short phrases. This may be too short, but we have been seeing AV-1's of 30 pages or more … without the findings. A good length for the main body of this document is 2-3 pages, with another 5-7 pages for the findings. If you need to add information, such as a description of your methodology, project plan or some other aspect of the architecture, simply include it as an appendix. This way the people who want to understand the essence of you architecture effort can obtain that information quickly and without having to wade through a lot of technobabble. Make sure you have some way to trace your findings back to specific architecture products. That information should be in the AV-2 as well.

---

[28] DoD Architecture Framework v. 1.0, 9 February 2004, Volume II, p. 3-2

[29] DoD Architecture Framework v. 1.0, 9 February 2004, Deskbook, p. 2-31

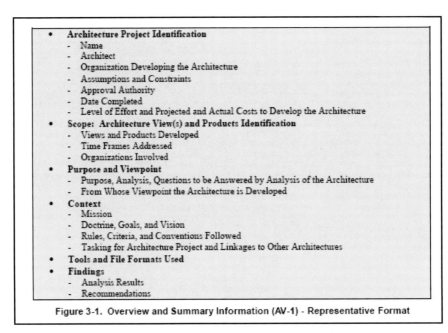

Figure 3-1. Overview and Summary Information (AV-1) - Representative Format

Figure 2-12. The executive summary of your architecture.

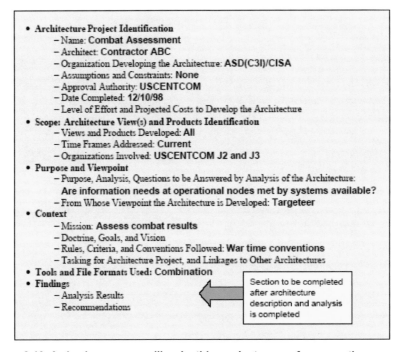

Figure 2-13. A simple response will make this product more of an executive summary.

AV-2 – Your Definitions

As we noted above, the AV-2 contains much more than a "dictionary" or glossary. As stated in the DoDAF, in the AV-2 "each labeled graphical item (e.g., icon, box, or connecting line) in the graphical representation of an architectural product should have a corresponding entry in the

Integrated Dictionary."[30] It also consists of "textual definitions in the form of a glossary, a repository of architecture data, their taxonomies, and their metadata."[31] This means that the AV-2 is the complete database or repository of your architectural design. Although you can create a repository of flat files with a folder structure that includes the diagrams, it is much easier to use a strong database tool to capture the information as you go and have it associated directly with the objects in the diagram. Many tools provide this as a "description" attribute, as shown in Figure 2-14.

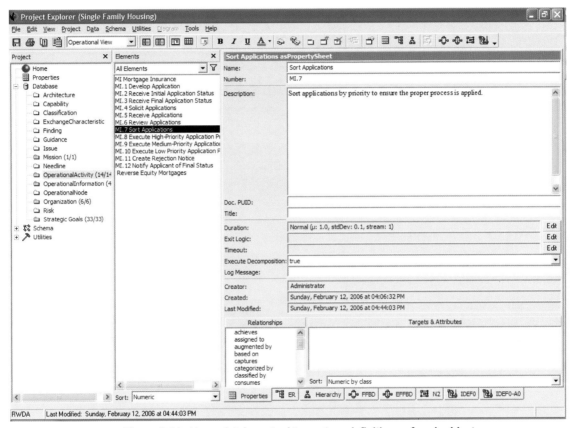

Figure 2-14. Use a database tool to capture definitions of each object.

The description of the AV-2 product also recommends that "Architects should use standard terms where possible."[32] You can find such standard terms in the DoDAF itself, Joint Publication 1 (JP-1), and many other standards. You will likely need to work with different communities that use the same term or phrase to mean different things (and of course use different terms for the same thing). Using these standard references

---

[30] DoD Architecture Framework v. 1.0, 9 February 2004, Volume II, p. 3-9

[31] DoD Architecture Framework v. 1.0, 9 February 2004, Volume II, p. 3-9

[32] DoD Architecture Framework v. 1.0, 9 February 2004, Volume II, p. 3-9

will help avoid miscommunication, but it will require work on the part of the architects. The biggest problem we've seen is the AV-2 being generated as a pure text document, decoupled for the database tool used. This situation often occurs because the architects don't fill in the descriptions as they go or don't use standard terms. You will save a lot of time, money, and grief if you just fill in those description fields as you go and generate the AV-2 from the database.

2.2.4 What Are the Operational View (OV) Products?

The OVs focus on the set of information usually needed by personnel who plan and conduct operations, sometimes called the "business processes."[33] Since the operations related directly to the mission and capabilities, many architects develop these products first.

Hi-level Operational Concept Graphic (OV-1)

The OV-1 is probably the most familiar to those of us in the DOD community. After all, PowerPoint is considered the number one system engineering tool, at least within the beltway. The unofficial name for this product is "the cartoon." Figure 2-15 shows how the template was depicted in the predecessor to the DoDAF.[34]

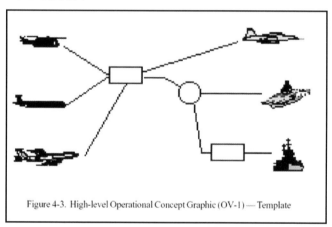

Figure 2-15. "The Cartoon" Template?

This "template" shows the external nodes as icons and internal systems or activities as boxes with lines of communication connecting them. Clearly this is a very abstract view of the diagram. It was removed from the

Figure 4-3. High-level Operational Concept Graphic (OV-1) — Template

DoDAF as it really doesn't express the form or substance of what the diagram is trying to communicate.

We joke about this graphic, but it's probably one of the most important, as it will portray the lasting image of your architecture. It also is the one diagram that will communicate the best to the widest audience. So you need to take some time to develop a very good one. Let's look at some examples.

---

[33] Using the term business process for warfighter operations doesn't appear, in our opinion, appropriate. Since DoD does have business processes (and is developing a Business Enterprise Architecture), you may want to use the more general term: operations.

[34] C4ISR Architecture Framework, Version 2.0, 18 December 1997, p. 4-8

The C4ISR AF quickly showed several examples. The one in Figure 2-16 provides a very interesting picture as an example of Theater Air Defense.[35] I often ask this question at my DoDAF classes, "What's the most important element of this diagram?" We get all kinds of answers for the satellite to the lightning bolts. We then say, "It must be the *state vector*, since that's the only words on the diagram." But the real answer is we don't know. That's because we don't have the accompanying text,[36] as required by the DoDAF (and its predecessor) which describes this picture. *Hence, we only have half the story with the diagram.*

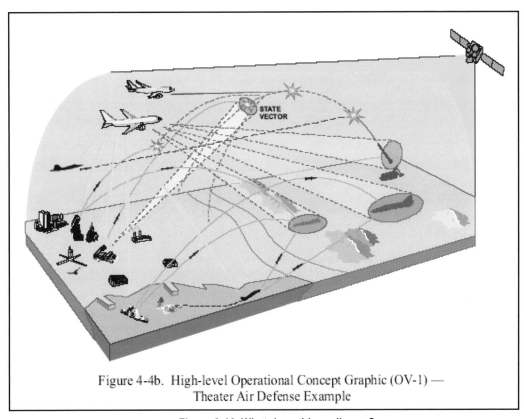

Figure 4-4b. High-level Operational Concept Graphic (OV-1) —
Theater Air Defense Example

Figure 2-16. What does this really say?

Although they say a picture is worth a thousand words, in our experience, we've found that it takes a thousand words to describe most pictures.

You also may find you need a number of pictures, not just one, to fully describe your architecture. For example, if you looked at the picture developed for the Financial Management Enterprise Architecture

---

[35] C4ISR Architecture Framework, Version 2.0, 18 December 1997, p. 4-10

[36] "A textual description accompanying the graphic is crucial. Graphics alone are not sufficient for capturing necessary architecture data." DoD Architecture Framework v. 1.0, 9 February 2004, Volume II, p. 4-1

(not all the Business Enterprise Architecture), shown in Figure 2-17,[37] even with the description (which we wrote for it), you would probably not understand the specific scenarios that have been brought together in this one, overarching graphic.

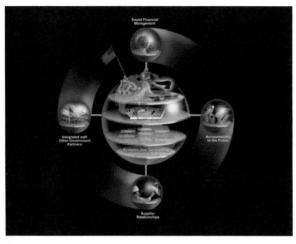

Figure 2-17. The "To-Be" View of the FMEA depicted the bringing together of the DoD Business Processes into a common DoD framework.

An interesting note, in Volume I of the DoDAF, they describe the set of products for the integrated architecture. This product set is similar to the C4ISR AF's "essential products," except that it replaces the OV-1 with the OV-5. Where we think the OV-5 is important, the OV-1 is critical to the number one mission of architectures: communication.

Operational Node Connectivity (OV-2)

The next OV product is the OV-2, which captures information about the operational nodes, how they need to communicate (logical interfaces or needlines), and information that needs to be exchanged between those nodes (Information Exchange Requirements – IER). You can also associate the operational activities with the operational nodes (see Figure 2-18 for the sample template[38]).

You can see that this diagram looks like a more abstract depiction of the OV-1. In fact it is it can be that and more. If you replaced the boxes with icons of the things they represent and the needlines with lightning bolts or some other means to show a logical interface (as usually we don't specify the connections in the OV-1 to the level of a physical interface – see SV-6 discussion), then we have similar pictures. Hence, this is why a lot of people have begun to think that the OV-1 cartoon is not so important (which we disagree for the reasons stated above).

---

[37] This diagram was previously available on the FMEA/BMMP website http//www.dod.mil/comptroller/bmmp/pages/index.html. This website has since been removed. BEA is now part of the Defense Business Transformation Agency (circa 2006).

[38] DoD Architecture Framework v. 1.0, 9 February 2004, Volume II, p. 4-9

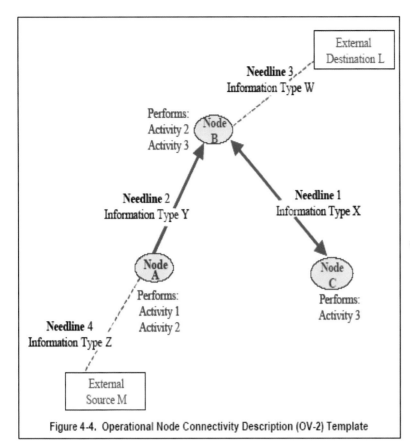

Figure 4-4. Operational Node Connectivity Description (OV-2) Template

Figure 2-18. OV-2 – A more abstract view of the operations.

However, the OV-2 adds the information about the information types and relates them to the activities. However, in practice, there usually isn't enough room to put the activities and even the information types.

Figure 2-19 shows an example of the OV-2, from the Framework.[39] In this example they have included the activities and information, but it makes the diagram look fairly busy. You might want to present something like this with overlays to show the overall needlines, then the information exchanged, then finally the activities.

The OV-2 is also where the DoDAF begins to show their versions of Unified Modeling Language (UML) diagrams. These diagrams are included to show that other techniques (beyond structured analysis) are acceptable. Figure 2-20 shows the UML-like diagram for the OV-2.[40] Note the major difference appears to be replacing node boxes with stick figures. We haven't found this particular diagram in any book on UML, but it does give you the idea you can use other techniques.

---

[39] DoD Architecture Framework v. 1.0, 9 February 2004, Deskbook, p. 2-33

[40] DoD Architecture Framework v. 1.0, 9 February 2004, Volume II, p. 4-11

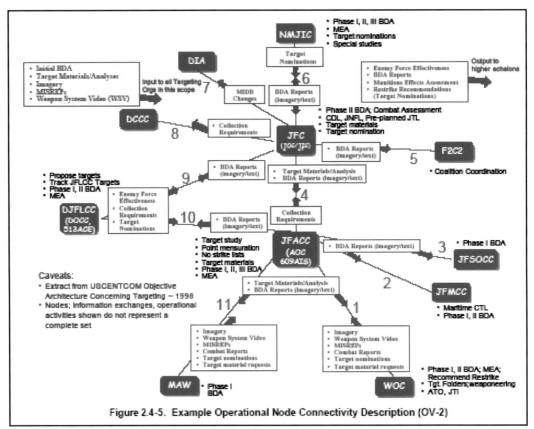

Figure 2.4-5. Example Operational Node Connectivity Description (OV-2)

Figure 2-19. Too busy?

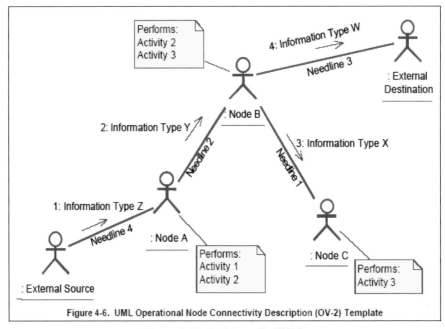

Figure 4-6. UML Operational Node Connectivity Description (OV-2) Template

(Analogous to Fig 2-18) — **Figure 2-20. Is this really UML?**

no, but it tries to make a point

Operational Information Exchange Matrix (OV-3)

The OV-3 (whose template is shown in Figure 2-21[41]) provides a very detailed set of information about the operational interfaces. To completely create these diagrams, you may find having and 11"x17" printer or plotter very helpful. Notice how it ties together the nodes, activities, and information flow more completely. The only thing you don't get out of this diagram, which the OV-2 provides, is the sense of flow. For simple operational scenarios, building this table by hand is feasible, but as you get to more complex situations you will find that having a tool generate this matrix (and keep it in synch with the other diagrams – OV-2 and OV-5 in particular) will be much easier. I have seen it tried the manual way on a large enterprise architecture project and the effort it took was substantial.

Needline Identifier	Information Exchange Identifier	Information Element Description					Producer		Consumer	
		Information Element Name and Identifier	Content	Scope	Accuracy	Language	Sending Op Node Name and Identifier	Sending Op Activity Name and Identifier	Receiving Op Node Name and Identifier	Receiving Op Activity Name and Identifier

Needline Identifier	Information Exchange Identifier	Nature of Transaction					Performance Attributes		Information Assurance			Security			
		Mission/Scenario UJTL or METL	Transaction Type	Triggering Event	Interoperability Level Required	Criticality	Periodicity	Timeliness	Access Control	Availability	Confidentiality	Dissemination Control	Integrity	Accountability	Protection (Type Name, Duration, Date)	Classification	Classification Caveat

Figure 4-8. Operational Information Exchange Matrix (OV-3) – Template

Figure 2-21. Don't try to generate this in Microsoft Word.

Figure 2-22 shows an example of this DoDAF product.[42] It doesn't include all the columns, thus it fits on a page and can still be read. Notice also that they continue the practice of just providing a number for the needline. You may want to label the needlines by the beginning and ending node name to make it easier to know what nodes it connects.

---

[41] DoD Architecture Framework v. 1.0, 9 February 2004, Volume II, p. 4-17

[42] DoD Architecture Framework v. 1.0, 9 February 2004, Deskbook, p. 2-34

		Information Element Description					Producer		Consumer		Nature of Transaction				
Needline Identifier	Information Exchange Identifier	Information Element Name and Identifier	Content	Scope	Accuracy	Language	Sending Op Node Name and Identifier	Sending Op Activity Name and Identifier	Receiving Op Node Name and Identifier	Receiving Op Activity Name and Identifier	Mission / Scenario UJTL or METL	Transaction Type	Triggering Event	Interoperability Level Required	Criticality
1	WOC-JFAC C1	BDA Report	Report on Battle Damage	Theater	1 Day	English	WOC	Conduct Battle Damage Assessment	JFACC	Conduct Munitions Effects Assessment	Combat Assessment	Collab-orate	Air Strike 072200, 0615am	2A	High
1	WOC-JFAC C2	Target Nomin-ations	Report on Possible Targets	Theater	2 Hours	English	WOC	Recommend Restrike	JFACC	Request Target Materials	Combat Assessment	Direct	AirTO XX, 072300	1B	High
2															
...															
11	MAW-JFAC C1	BDA Report	Report on Battle Damage	Theater	1 Day	English	MAW	Conduct Battle Damage Assessment	JFACC	Conduct Munitions Effects Assessment	Combat Assessment	Collab-orate	Air Strike 072200, 0615am	2A	High

Figure 2.4-6. Notional Operational Information Exchange Matrix (OV-3)

Figure 2-22. A subset of the complete OV-3.

Organizational Relationships Chart (OV-4)

The OV-4 diagram (see Figure 2-23[43]) should look familiar. It's simply an organization chart with solid lines connecting the boxes to show the reporting chain and dashed lines to show coordination between groups.

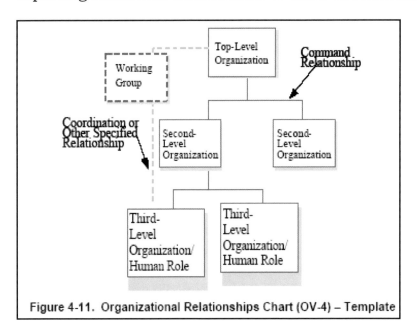

Figure 4-11. Organizational Relationships Chart (OV-4) – Template

Figure 2-23. OV-4 –A typical organization chart.

---

[43] DoD Architecture Framework v. 1.0, 9 February 2004, Volume II, p. 4-28

The DoDAF also includes a UML-like version of the organization chart, as shown in Figure 2-24,[44] but it doesn't seem to represent a standard UML diagram. The description has it as a cross between a class diagram and the use case diagram (which uses the stick figures as "actor" icons). Since the organization chart (see example in Figure 2-25[45]) is a standard chart instantly recognizable by almost everyone, we recommend sticking with it.

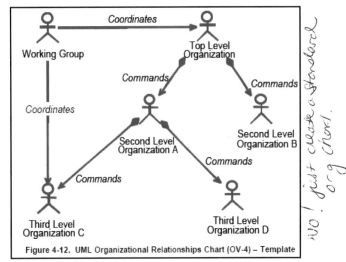

Figure 4-12. UML Organizational Relationships Chart (OV-4) – Template

No! just create a standard org chart.

Figure 2-24. Another UML-like view.

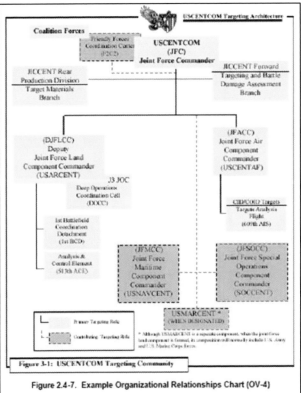

Figure 2.4-7. Example Organizational Relationships Chart (OV-4)

Figure 2-25. A more typical example.

---

[44] DoD Architecture Framework v. 1.0, 9 February 2004, Volume II, p. 4-28

[45] DoD Architecture Framework v. 1.0, 9 February 2004, Deskbook, p. 2-35

Operational Activity Model (OV-5)

This product actually contains two diagrams (see Figure 2-26[46]): one depicts the hierarchy of operational activities, and the other shows the informational flow between operational activities. This product is one of the most important diagrams in the architecture and is included in the DoDAF's definition of an integrated architecture. We have designated the hierarchy chart the OV-5a and the flow diagram as the OV-5b. The DoDAF does not use these designations in Version 1.0, but you might find it useful. The complete product requires both diagrams. However, many people forget about the hierarchy chart, which causes some confusion as you will likely produce many OV-5b diagrams, one for each level of decomposition.

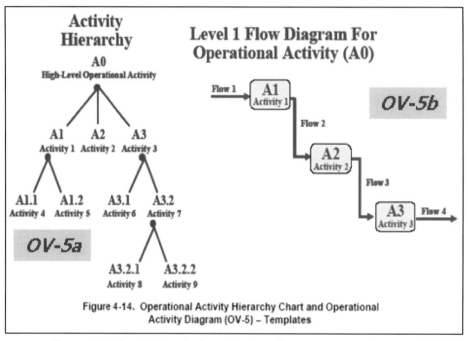

Figure 4-14. Operational Activity Hierarchy Chart and Operational Activity Diagram (OV-5) – Templates

Figure 2-26. The OV-5 product contains two diagram types, not just one.

In fact, you may find that you need to produce 10s to 100s of OV-5b diagrams to completely capture all the facets of your operational activities. The potentially large number of diagrams can become overwhelming. In Chapters 5 and 6, we will provide some insights into when to stop the decomposition process to end up with a sufficient number of diagrams, without breaking you budget.

The DoDAF also recommends using this diagram to convey more information. For example, you could estimate the costs of each activity and display them on this chart. Or you could annotate the activities with the operational nodes the implement these activities. You could even

---

[46] DoD Architecture Framework v. 1.0, 9 February 2004, Volume II, p. 4-33

color code them to show critical path activities or problem areas or even new tasks that are needed for your future architecture.

An example of an OV-5b can be seen in Figure 2-27.[47] This diagram uses the Integration Definition (IDEF) technique to depict the activities. This rather busy diagram only shows data flows between functions (operational activities). No sequencing information is in this model, although many people think it is implied. Other structured analysis techniques could also be used (such as a Yourdon data flow diagram or N2 chart).

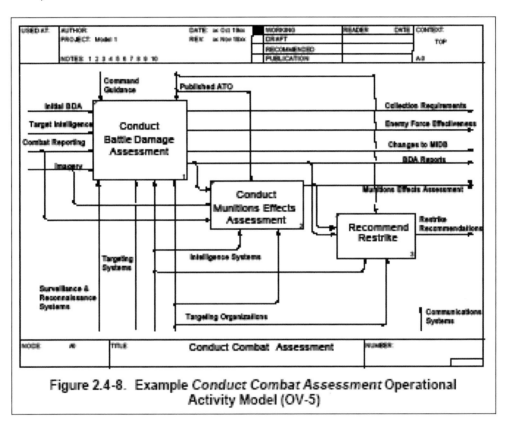

Figure 2.4-8. Example *Conduct Combat Assessment* Operational Activity Model (OV-5)

Figure 2-27. An OV-5 example using an IDEF 0 diagram.

The DoDAF also shows an OV-5 as a UML view. They chose to associate the use case diagram and activity model to represent with the operational activity information flows. Figure 2-28 shows the use case diagram equivalent to the OV-5b.[48] Neither this diagram nor the activity model replaces the need for a hierarchy diagram (the OV-5a). Since it can include the method inheritance, you might consider applying the use case diagram to show hierarchy, which could be considered roughly the equivalent of the operational activities (again a rather loose interpretation of UML vs. the standard structure analysis approach).

---

[47] DoD Architecture Framework v. 1.0, 9 February 2004, Deskbook, p. 2-36

[48] DoD Architecture Framework v. 1.0, 9 February 2004, Volume II, p. 4-35

Note that this diagram and the activity model contain the information about the associated nodes. This fact points to the concern many system engineers have about UML – it defines the objects first, rather than focusing on the functions and keeping the functional analysis "pure." We think you just need to be consistent in applying your chosen technique and let the products fall out from your methodology. In other words, do what works best for you and your customers.

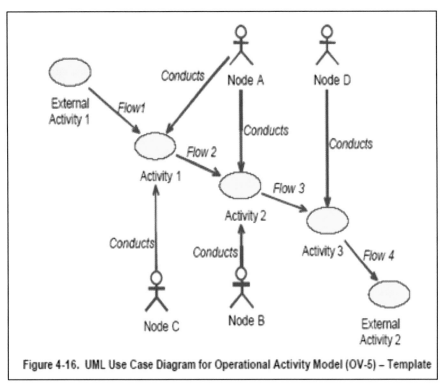

Figure 4-16. UML Use Case Diagram for Operational Activity Model (OV-5) – Template

Figure 2-28. Part of the UML approach to defining the OV-5.

Operational Activity Sequence and Timing Descriptions (OV-6)

The OV-6 provides three optional diagram approaches to capturing the timing and sequencing information of the operational activities. The three are:

- OV-6a – Operational Rules Model
- OV-6b – Operational State Transition Description
- OV-6c – Operational Event-Trace Description

These diagrams represent three *different* ways to get at the timing and sequencing. They do not all need to be done and they are not the only ways of showing this information. They do tend to be rather static depictions of the operational activity dynamics (if that sounds like an oxymoron it probably is). The DoDAF does discuss the way to get to an executable architecture, using modeling and simulation techniques, such as Colored PetriNets (CPN).[49] Other M&S techniques, such as discrete event simulation and Monte Carlo simulations can also be used. We will address the methods for creating executable architectures in more depth in Chapter 5, but for now, let's look at each of the three versions of the OV-6 product.

OV-6a – Operational Rules Model

The OV-6a captures the operational or "business" rules as they constrain an enterprise, mission, operation, business, or architecture. These rules (or we may think of them as policies) are usually captured in some simple language or structured logic statements, as can be seen from the example[50] below:

> - ATOs are developed on a 24- to 96-hour planning cycle.
> - BDAs are developed for every target that has had an air sortie directed against it.
> - MEAs are developed to identify deficiencies in weapon system/munitions performance, tactics, or aim point selection.

These statements have also been called functional requirements or performance specifications and provide some information about the timing and sequencing of the functions. Other forms of the OV-6a include a decision or fault tree, entity-relationship diagrams, and detailed, testable requirements statements.

As the statements become more complex and interactive with one another, this technique proves very limited. In particular, when an operation transfers states, we need a different approach.

OV-6b – Operational State Transition Description

When the operational situation changes from peacetime to alert or alert to attack, we need some way to show what triggers these changes of state and what happens as a result. The state transition diagram (STD) provides a graphical way of describing how an operational node or activity responds to various events by changing its state. Figure 2-29 shows an example from the Framework of a state transition diagram.[51] The way this diagram is often used, it doesn't provide a clear linkage to the functions (operational activities) and data (operational information elements). The "triggering" events shown in this figure (e.g., "mobilized") often can not be traced back to a function in the OV-5 or a data element that triggers the state change. That's because in the generalized formulation of the STD, the transition between states is characterized by

---

[49] DoD Architecture Framework v. 1.0, 9 February 2004, Volume II, p. 4-50

[50] DoD Architecture Framework v. 1.0, 9 February 2004, Deskbook, p. 2-37

[51] DoD Architecture Framework v. 1.0, 9 February 2004, Deskbook, p. 2-38

conditions and actions,[52] which may not be the same as a function or data. However, if you use functions and data, the same ones as on the OV-5, you obtain the linkage between the diagrams that is needed to begin to capture the dynamics. However, even when properly applied, the STD still doesn't deal well with more complex interactions between functions and data. The event-trace diagram is another technique for trying to articulate the timing and sequencing to avoid some of these problems.

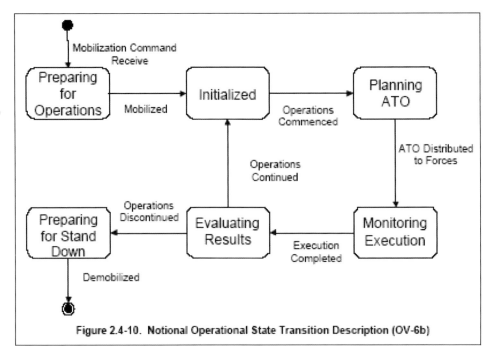

Figure 2.4-10. Notional Operational State Transition Description (OV-6b)

Figure 2-29. How are these linked to functions and data?

OV-6c – Operational Event-Trace Description

The OV-6c uses the event-trace diagram technique to capture time-ordered information exchanges between operational nodes. This technique has been used for sometime in the structured analysis world, but has gained prominence by it's incorporation in the UML technique as the "sequence diagram."[53] These diagrams are in heavy use today in many of the architecture projects in an attempt to get at the "process flow" of the operational activities. Unfortunately, most of these diagrams are still developed in drawing tools, which do not enforce the proper use of the diagrams.

---

[52] Modern Structured Analysis, Edward Yourdon, Prentice-Hall, Inc., 1989, p. 265

[53] Understanding UML – The Developer's Guide with a Web-based Application in Java, Paul Harmon and Mark Watson, Morgan Kaufmann Publishers, Inc., 1998, p.201-206

Figure 2-30 shows and example from the Framework of the OV-6c.[54] We see the operational nodes and "events" occurring between these nodes to transfer the action from one node to another. Whereas this gives us some idea for the sequencing of events in a particular scenario, how are these events related to the functions and data in the OV-5? Also, how can we get timing information out of them, again linked directly to the functions and data?

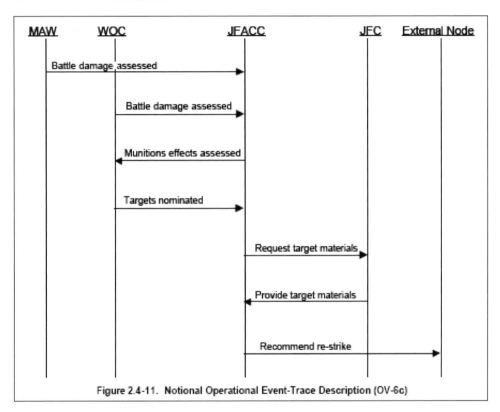

Figure 2.4-11. Notional Operational Event-Trace Description (OV-6c)

Figure 2-30. Again where's the linkage between this diagram and the OV-5?

In summary, all the OV-6 diagrams have a very poor linkage between the operational activities and information portrayed in the OV-5. They also do not capture the necessary set of information, in particular the logical sequencing, of anything but simple dynamics. This later problem is a fundamental problem with the technique, not just a practitioner problem. We will discuss this in more depth in Chapter 5 as we talk about other techniques and executable architectures.

Logical Data Model (OV-7)

The last of the OVs is the OV-7. The logical data model describes the data elements at a high level of abstraction, but not the highest. Most data modelers suggest creating a *conceptual* data model first. The conceptual data model is a list of the data elements of critical interest to

---

[54] DoD Architecture Framework v. 1.0, 9 February 2004, Deskbook, p. 2-39

the enterprise. This list is separated into different categories or classifications. Classification systems,[55] such as the ones used in biology and chemistry, gather information into "bins" or in database terminology, schemas. The relationships between the classes of data can then be captured in a structured language, such as was shown in the OV-6a.

Once the list of data elements and its classification scheme have been developed, you can depict the data elements, their attributes, and relationships in an *entity-relationship-attribute* (ERA) diagram, as shown in Figure 2-31.[56] We often use the word *element* as a synonym for *entity* in discussing this diagram.

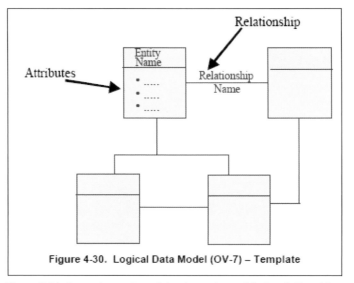

Figure 4-30. Logical Data Model (OV-7) – Template

Figure 2-31. A way to capture data elements and their relationships. *ERA diagram*

Note that this technique can be used to diagram sentences, where the entity is a noun, the relationship represents the verb, and the attributes are similar to adjectives (they modify the noun/entity). What's missing for this? *Adverbs*. You may find it useful to include attributes on the relationships as well. We will discuss another technique in Chapter 5 that applies this idea. Figure 2-32 provides an example of an ERA diagram.[57]

UML also has an equivalent to this diagram: the class diagram. Class diagrams, as shown in Figure 2-33,[58] provide many of the same characteristics as the ERA, with a couple important additions. The lower lines in the boxes (below the attributes) provide a place to collected

---

[55] See *Building Enterprise Information Architectures* by Melissa A. Cook, 1996, Prentice-Hall, Inc. for more information on classification systems and data modeling.

[56] DoD Architecture Framework v. 1.0, 9 February 2004, Volume II, p. 4-63

[57] DoD Architecture Framework v. 1.0, 9 February 2004, Deskbook, p. 2-40

[58] DoD Architecture Framework v. 1.0, 9 February 2004, Volume II, p. 4-63

methods. Methods are used to manage the operations related to an object's attributes. We used to call these "subroutines" procedural code development, but subroutines could be used in other ways. In object-oriented programming, the objects (or entities) encapsulate the attributes and methods and determine how other objects can access these features.

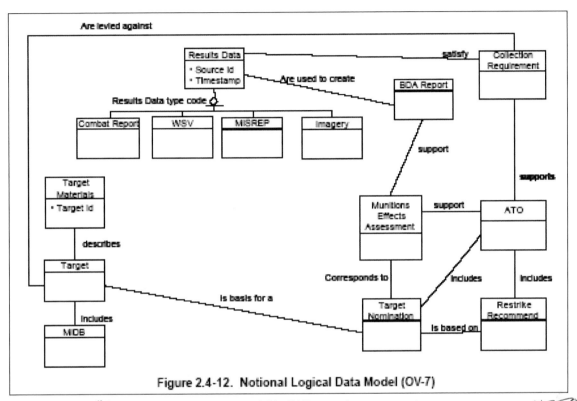

Figure 2.4-12. Notional Logical Data Model (OV-7)

ERA diagram 2 **Figure 2-32. OV-7 example.**

In addition, the class diagram allows "inheritance" where objects that are children of the parent object inherit its attributes and methods. The ERA diagram does not provide this important feature.

Now that we've completed the OVs, let's see what the system views do for us.

methods?

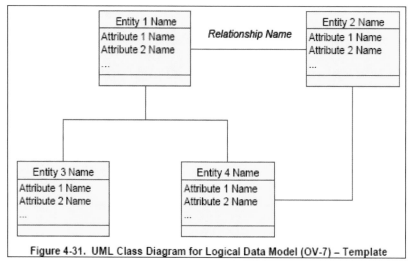

Figure 4-31. UML Class Diagram for Logical Data Model (OV-7) – Template

Figure 2-33. ERD on steroids? *Class Diagram*

2.2.5 What Are the System View (SV) Products?

The SVs focus on the implementation of the business processes captured in the OVs. You will see that the type of information captured is very similar to the OVs, but at a lower level of detail. Many consider the OV information as the *requirements* for the SVs.

System Interface Description (SV-1)

The first of the SVs is the system interface description shown in Figure 2-34.[59] The nodes shown are system nodes, which can include facilities, organizations, buildings, and bases. You can make the system nodes the same as the operational nodes, as shown in the example in Figure 2-35.[60] If you don't you may want to create a table that relates the system nodes to the operational nodes, although there is no such product in the Framework.

this sounds like it would be a best practice

Notice how similar this diagram is to the OV-2. It contains nodes, interfaces (similar to needlines) and system functions (similar to the operational activities). The major difference is to show the packaging of functions as systems.

Clearly this diagram by itself doesn't completely specify the interfaces between systems, since it does not include the data elements that flow over the interface. You will want to include this information in any modeling, as it will be needed for SV-6 matrix.

---

[59] DoD Architecture Framework v. 1.0, 9 February 2004, Volume II, p. 5-4

[60] DoD Architecture Framework v. 1.0, 9 February 2004, Deskbook, p. 2-41

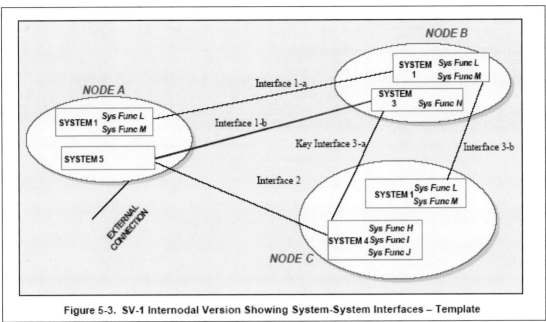

Figure 5-3. SV-1 Internodal Version Showing System-System Interfaces – Template

Figure 2-34. The systems equivalent to the OV-2. See p. 41 for operational Node Connectivity Template

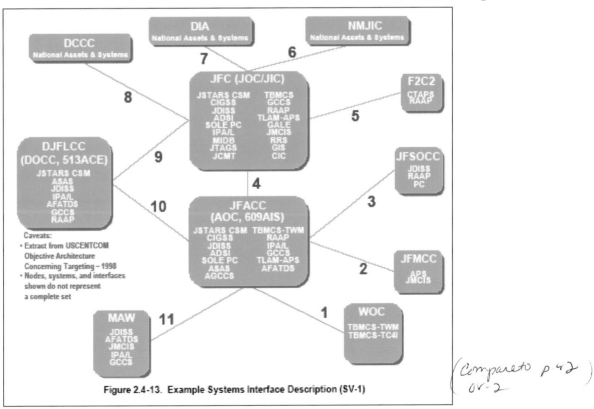

Figure 2.4-13. Example Systems Interface Description (SV-1)

(Compare to p. 42) OV-2

Figure 2-35. You may have to supplement this diagram to obtain all the necessary information.

The example in Figure 2-35 demonstrates how difficult it is to put all the information suggested in the template into a diagram. If you tried to include the system functions for all the systems listed in these nodes (organizations) the chart would be unreadable. Hence you may need additional SV-1s at a more detailed level and/or include the information in other products, such as the SV-6.

The UML equivalent for the SV-1 can be seen in Figure 2-36.[61] The DoDAF uses the combination of the UML *component* and *deployment diagrams* to represent the information needed for the SV-1. The deployment portion shows the nodes as three-dimensional boxes with the interfaces linking the nodes. The systems are shown using the component diagram notation. It includes a callout for the system functions as well to complete the SV-1 information content. Please note, you can also show system to system links in this diagram as well (instead of the node-to-node links shown in the figure).

Again, the use of UML here may be most appropriate in creating a software architecture or diagrams that will go to software developers. Others might find this portrayal of the SV-1 confusing. Chose whichever works best for you audience.

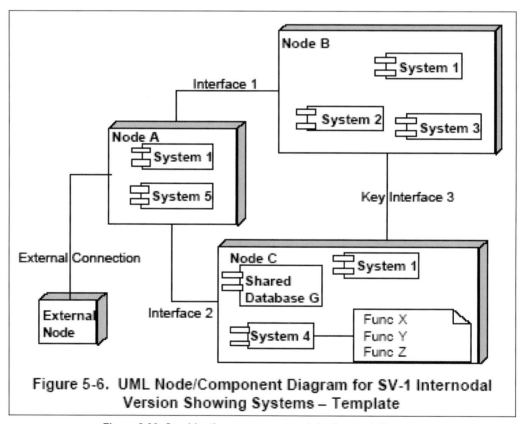

Figure 5-6. UML Node/Component Diagram for SV-1 Internodal Version Showing Systems – Template

Figure 2-36. Combination component and deployment diagram.

[61] DoD Architecture Framework v. 1.0, 9 February 2004, Volume II, p. 5-6

Systems Communications Description (SV-2)

The SV-2 looks somewhat similar to the SV-1. It shows the nodes connected by the detailed communications interfaces, as shown in Figure 2-37.[62] In fact, you might say that the SV-2 is simply a decomposition of the communications infrastructure, which many be an important aspect of your architecture, particularly in a net-centric environment.

We can speculate as to why there are two similar products,[63] but you can use this second product to highlight the critical communications elements of you architecture. Many customers (NSA and DISA for example) are very concerned about the communications infrastructure and its impacts on security and information assurance. Since they will be looking for both, you might want to have both an SV-1 and SV-2 for those customers.

 In the example of the SV-2 shown in Figure 2-38[64] we can see that the only difference between this diagram and the SV-1 is that they have specified the communications paths. So however you label these diagrams, you will want to capture the important aspects of communications, where they are appropriate.

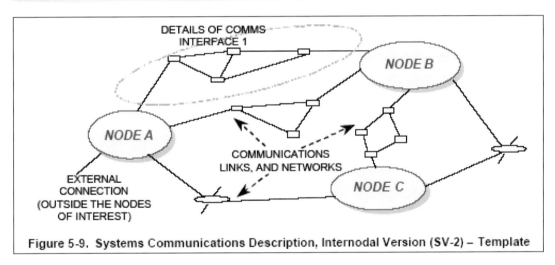

Figure 5-9. Systems Communications Description, Internodal Version (SV-2) – Template

Figure 2-37. Same as the SV-1?

---

[62] DoD Architecture Framework v. 1.0, 9 February 2004, Volume II, p. 5-13

[63] The original C4ISR Architecture Framework, Version 1.0 and most of the drafts of 2.0 had a diagram similar to the OV-1 as the SV-1 and the SV-2 and OV-2 we seen as equivalents. It appears that someone decided that they didn't need two cartoons before 2.0 went final and instead of renumbering all the SVs, decided to invent the SV-2.

[64] DoD Architecture Framework v. 1.0, 9 February 2004, Deskbook, p. 2-42

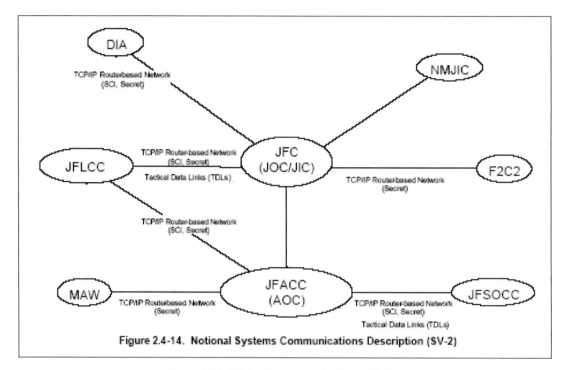

Figure 2.4-14. Notional Systems Communications Description (SV-2)

Figure 2-38. SV-1 with communications labels?

Systems-Systems Matrix (SV-3)

The SV-3 shows the interfaces between systems in the form of a matrix (see Figure 2-39).[65] This form allows a quick overview of all the interface characteristics that we provided in the SV-1s, but may not be as obvious, such as the rapid assessment of potential commonalities and redundancies (or, if fault-tolerance is desired, the lack of redundancies).

	SYSTEM 1	SYSTEM 2	SYSTEM 3	SYSTEM 4	SYSTEM 5	SYSTEM 6	SYSTEM 7	SYSTEM 8	SYSTEM 9	SYSTEM 10
SYSTEM 1		●								
SYSTEM 2	●		●	●	●	●				
SYSTEM 3		●		●	●	●				
SYSTEM 4		●	●		●	●				
SYSTEM 5		●	●	●		●				
SYSTEM 6	●	●	●	●	●		●	●	●	●
SYSTEM 7						●				
SYSTEM 8						●				
SYSTEM 9						●				
SYSTEM 10						●				

Figure 5-12. Systems-Systems Matrix (SV-3) – Template

Figure 2-39. Systems-Systems Matrix (SV-3) – Template.

Another form of this matrix is called an "N2" (pronounced N-square) chart, where the systems are instead placed in the diagonal gray boxes. The N2 form (also used for functions) shows the data elements

---

65 DoD Architecture Framework v. 1.0, 9 February 2004, Volume II, p. 5-21

transferred between each of the systems, thus providing more information about the interfaces than the SV-3 above.

In fact, you can improve the usefulness of this diagram by adding a variety of information in the off-diagonal elements of the matrix. Figure 2-40 shows an example from the C4ISR Architecture Framework[66] that uses the off-diagonal elements to show both existing and planned interfaces. You can also substitute a color coding to show this same kind of information.

Also consider putting schedule, performance, or cost information in the off-diagonals. Those parameters hold significant interest to most decision makers. You can easily see how adding information to some of these diagrams can improve their use in communicating the results of the architecture. Don't feel that the Framework limits you. It provides a good starting point for communication.

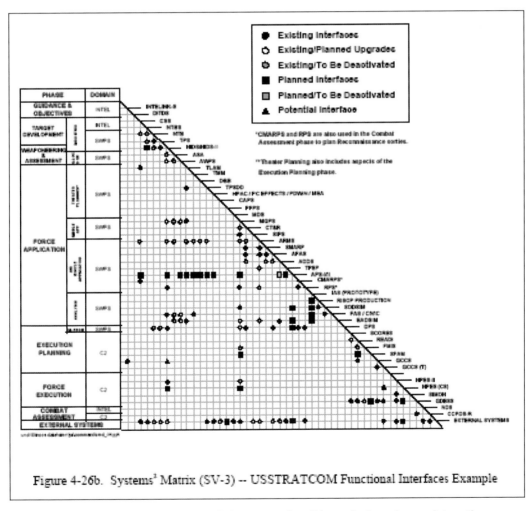

Figure 4-26b. Systems' Matrix (SV-3) -- USSTRATCOM Functional Interfaces Example

Figure 2-40. Using the off-diagonal elements makes this product much more interesting.

---

[66] C4ISR Architecture Framework, Version 2.0, 18 December 1997, p. 4-6

hmmm... Mankitis [part of the framework? Attributes in DoDAF's

Systems Functionality Description (SV-4)

Just like the OV-5, the SV-4 comes with two diagrams: 1) the functional hierarchy and 2) the data flow diagram. Figures 2-41 and 2-42 show each of them.[67] For easy reference, I call the hierarchy chart SV-4a and the data flow chart SV-4b, although no such designation is part of the Framework.

The SV-4a looks the same as the OV-5a. Both show the decomposition of higher level activities/functions. Each level provides more detail. If you take the approach that the system functions are simply a decomposition of the operational activities, you might want to work with these two together, not worrying about which is a system function and which is an operational activity until the end. If you take the other approach (where these are separate decompositions), then you will have two parallel decompositions. You can relate them to each other in the SV-5 product (see next section).

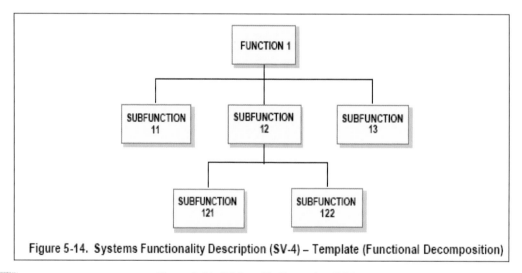

Figure 5-14. Systems Functionality Description (SV-4) – Template (Functional Decomposition)

Figure 2-41. SV-4a – Similar to the OV-5a.

The data flow diagram shown in Figure 2-42 provides the data flow between functions, much like the OV-5b. However, the form shown in the template comes from a specific technique: Yourdon-Demarco.[68]

Figure 2-43 shows an example of a data flow diagram using this technique.[69] Some evaluators will be looking for this diagram; others would expect you to use the same technique consistently throughout

---

[67] Both diagrams are from DoD Architecture Framework v. 1.0, 9 February 2004, Volume II, p. 5-26

[68] Modern Structured Analysis, Edward Yourdon, Prentice-Hall, Inc., 1989, p. 141

[69] C4ISR Architecture Framework, Version 2.0, 18 December 1997, p. 4-66

your architecture. Our recommendation is to do everything in the same technique and if a particular customer or evaluator wants to see it in this form then redraw it for them. It won't take that long and you will meet everyone's requirements.

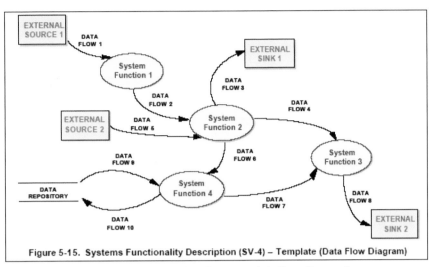

Figure 5-15. Systems Functionality Description (SV-4) – Template (Data Flow Diagram)

Figure 2-42. A Yourdon-Demarco data flow diagram?

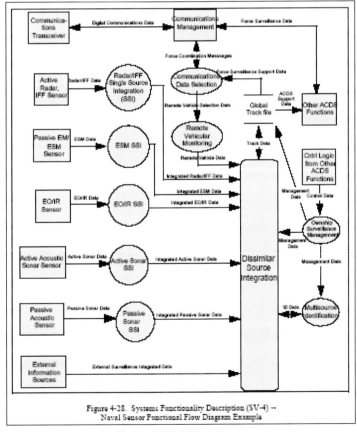

Figure 4-28. Systems Functionality Description (SV-4) --
Naval Sensor Functional Flow Diagram Example

Figure 2-43. DFD example.

Operational Activity to Systems Function Traceability Matrix (SV-5)

The next SV product provides the only explicit link between two views: operational and systems. The basic form of this matrix is simply a table with system functions as the rows and operational activities as columns, with the relationship between them shown as an "X." However, you can also do it at the planner level as shown in Figure 2-44.[70] The colored circles indicate capability of the system (red – planned; yellow – partial; green – full). It also shows how the operational activities form capabilities and the system functions create systems. All this information in a simple matrix form aids the decision maker. You can add costs to the circles (O&M and R&D) and thereby have both cost and schedule in the same diagram.

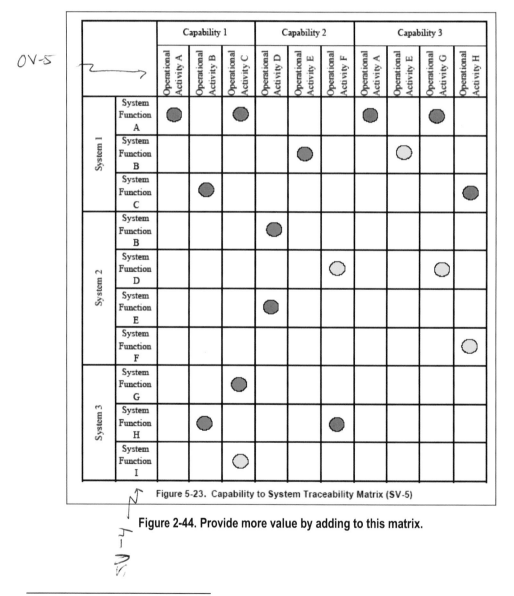

Figure 5-23. Capability to System Traceability Matrix (SV-5)

Figure 2-44. Provide more value by adding to this matrix.

---

[70] DoD Architecture Framework v. 1.0, 9 February 2004, Volume II, p. 5-37

Systems Data Exchange Matrix (SV-6)

The SV-6 looks a lot like the OV-3. As can be readily seen in Figure 2-45,[71] the SV-6 contains several more data description attributes than the OV-3 (*format type* and *media type*), as well as performance (*throughput* and *size*), but fundamentally they are the same. Please note, many of these additional attributes could have been expressed for the operational information as well, but the DoDAF recognizes that those elements will be more abstract. Linkages to standards also appear here (*data standards* and *security standards*). Hence, we could say that these should link to the TV-1 as well. You should read the information in Volume II carefully to use the correct inputs to this table. *SV-6 : OV-3/TV-1*

Interface Identifier	Data Exchange Identifier	Data Description							Producer		Consumer		Nature of Transaction		
System Interface Name and Identifier	System Data Exchange Name and Identifier	Data Element Name and Identifier	Content	Format Type	Media Type	Accuracy	Units of Measurement	Data Standard	Sending System Name and Identifier	Sending System Function Name and Identifier	Receiving System Name and Identifier	Receiving System Function Name and Identifier	Transaction Type	Triggering Event	Interoperability Level Achieved	Criticality

Interface Identifier	Data Exchange Identifier	Performance Attributes				Information Assurance							Security				
System Interface Name and Identifier	System Data Exchange Name and Identifier	Periodicity	Timeliness	Throughput	Size	Access Control	Availability	Confidentiality	Dissemination Control	Integrity	Non-Repudiation Producer	Non-Repudiation Consumer	Protection (Type Name, Duration, Date)	Classification	Classification Caveat	Releasability	Security Standard

Figure 5-25. Systems Data Exchange Matrix (SV-6) – Template

Figure 2-45. Check out DoDAF Volume II for details of these table elements.

Systems Performance Parameters Matrix (SV-7)

Since the DoDAF is designed to support architectures in every domain, they could not come up with a template that captured the full set of parameters for any project. So the DoDAF calls the SV-7 in Figure

---

[71] DoD Architecture Framework v. 1.0, 9 February 2004, Volume II, p. 5-42

2-46 a "notional example."[72] This really means you're on your own. As such, you should look at your domain and determine what key performance parameters describe your architecture elements. For example, in a communications architecture you will be interested in bandwidth, throughput, and latency. In an intelligence architecture, quantity, quality, and timeliness of information are often used as key parameters. In a missile system architecture, we worry about thrust, weight, size, form factors, and many other parameters.

Recognize that you will likely have thresholds (the range of acceptable values) and objectives (the ultimate goals of the architecture, which may never be achieved). You also want to capture the baseline (where you are today) to demonstrate that the cost of development provides sufficient benefit to warrant the expenditure. Spend time with the stakeholders and be sure that you capture their ideas on what constitute the parameters of interest. Notice also that the OV-3 and SV-6 give you some pretty good hints at attributes, at least for C4ISR systems.

	Performance Range (Threshold and Objective) Measures		
	Time$_0$ (Baseline Architecture Time Period)	Time$_1$	Time$_n$ (Target Architecture Time Period)
System Name			
Hardware Element 1			
Maintainability			
Availability			
System Initialization Time			
Architecture data Transfer Rate			
Program Restart Time			
S/W Element 1 / H/W Element 1			
Architecture Data Capacity (e.g., throughput or # of input types)			
Automatic Processing Responses (by input type, # processed/unit time)			
Operator Interaction Response Times (by type)			
Availability			
Effectiveness			
Mean Time Between S/W Failures			
Organic Training			
S/W Element 2 / H/W Element 1			
Hardware Element 2			

Figure 5-27. Systems Performance Parameters Matrix (SV-7) – Notional Example

Figure 2-46. You need to come up with your own way to show the performance parameters.

---

[72] DoD Architecture Framework v. 1.0, 9 February 2004, Volume II, p. 5-50

Systems Evolution Description (SV-8)

GED should have this, in addition to service views a la DoDAF 1.5

This product shows the evolution of the systems over the timeframe of the architecture. You want to have a plan for the transitioning of systems from the current baseline to the "to-be" architecture. The SV-8 provides this roadmap for the spiral, incremental or other lifecycle approach you want to take in the overall development. An example from the Framework is shown in Figure 2-47.[73] This diagram shows an evolutionary approach (vs. the incremental or "migration" path approach).

This product becomes a key element of the transition plan. To create it, you must have both an as-is and to-be architecture. We have seen attempts to create this in parallel with the development of these architectures. The result was characterized as a plan to write a transition plan. As we will discuss in Chapter 5, there is a sequencing of the architecture development that will benefit all participants.

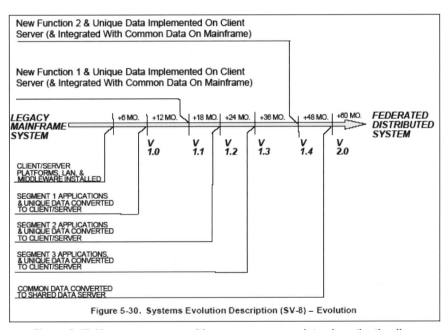

Figure 5-30. Systems Evolution Description (SV-8) – Evolution

Figure 2-47. You can come up with your own approach to show the timeline.

Systems Technology Forecast (SV-9)

The SV-9 shown in the Framework[74] (see Figure 2-48) is another "notional example." It must be related to information systems, since they are the only ones who think that long term is 12-18 months.

---

[73] DoD Architecture Framework v. 1.0, 9 February 2004, Volume II, p. 5-55

[74] DoD Architecture Framework v. 1.0, 9 February 2004, Volume II, p. 5-60

Table 5-9. Systems Technology Forecast (SV-9) – Notional Example

JTA Service	TECHNOLOGY FORECASTS		
	SHORT TERM (0-6 Months)	MID TERM (6-12 Months)	LONG TERM (12-18 Months)
Application Software			
Support Applications	Microsoft Office 2000 available (for Windows 2000)	Microsoft Office 2000 stable enough for full-scale implementation	Microsoft Office available for Linux E-mail on wireless PDAs commonplace
Application Platform			
Data Management	Oracle 9i available MySQL (Open Source DBMS) available		
Operating System		Next MS Windows desktop upgrade expected Next Red Hat Linux major release expected	Next MS Windows server upgrade expected
Physical Environment			Intel IA-64 becomes standard processor for desktops Initial use of quantum computing technologies
External Environment			
User Interface		Thin screen CRT monitors for PC desktops become price competitive	Thin screen LED monitors become price competitive for desktops Conventional CRT technology monitors for desktops become obsolete
Persistent Storage	5G PCMCIA type 2 card available		Disk storage capacity doubles again
Communications Networks		Cable modem service available for most telecommuting staff	Fiber optic connections available for most telecommuting staff

Figure 2-48. Another Notional Example.

I recommend adding the information from the SV-9 into the SV-8. This combined diagram provides the technology roadmap that will enable you to better communicate the technology insertions needed over the timeframe of the architecture. This approach also ensures that the two diagrams remain in synch. We also recommend that the SV-9 be part of the Transition Plan. The table form will provide details of the technology for insertion and can evaluate alternatives as they emerge.

Systems Functionality Sequence and Timing Descriptions (SV-10 a, b & c)   *Compare to OV-6*

Well as Yogi Berea said, "this is Deja Vu all over again." The products for timing and sequencing (see Figures 2-49, 2-50 and 2-51)[75] are similar to the OV-6 products, but at a more detailed level. This product set focuses on the constraints, timing and sequencing for systems, system components, and system functions.

> *If* field A *in* FORM-X *is set to* value T,
> *Then* field B *in* FORM-Y *must be set to* value T
> *And* field C *in* FORM-Z *must be set to* value T
> *End If*

Figure 5-34. Systems Rules Model (SV-10a) – Action Assertion Example

Figure 2-49. Captures constraints.

---

[75] DoD Architecture Framework v. 1.0, 9 February 2004, Volume II, p. 5-68, 5-71 & 5-75 respectively

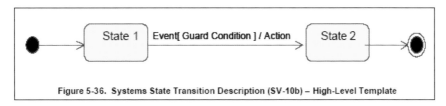

Figure 2-50. Sequencing of states and modes.

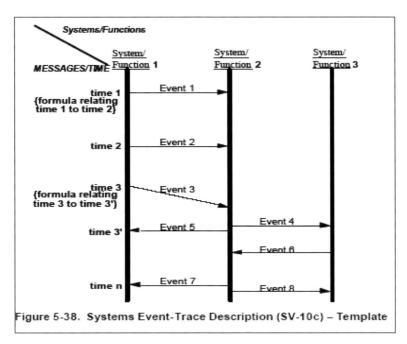

Figure 2-51. Timing and sequencing of systems/functions.

The limitations on these diagrams are the same as the ones we discussed above for the OV-6. In Chapter 5 we will discover a different way to capture timing and sequencing that's simpler and executable.

Physical Schema (SV-11)

The last of the SV products is the SV-11. Figure 2-52[76] shows different approaches to expressing the physical schema, from a specific message format to data definition language (DDL, such as structured query language – SQL).

Recently DoD has been emphasizing the use of Extensible Markup Language (XML) to capture physical schemas. A DoD XML Registry is maintained by the Defense Information Systems Agency (DISA). Although XML may require too much overhead for real-time systems, it still provides a simple means of expressing the information, so you may want to consider it as a means to document the physical schema.

---

[76] DoD Architecture Framework v. 1.0, 9 February 2004, Volume II, p. 5-79

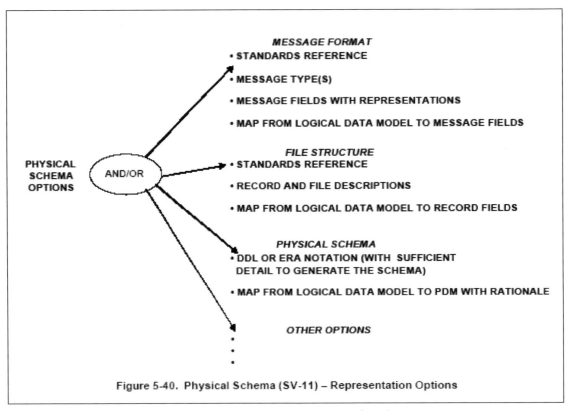

Figure 5-40. Physical Schema (SV-11) – Representation Options

Figure 2-52. Options, but XML is preferred.

2.2.6 What Are the Technical Standards View (TV) Products?

The last set of views capture the architecture's standards. The focus has been on technical standards, which most people interpret to mean hardware/software standards. However, since the TVs also link to the OVs, you need to consider including operational standards as well. In the DoDAF documentation, the only operational view they mention is the OV-7, thus relating it to data standards, but as we discussed earlier in this chapter you should consider process standards when developing the operational views.

Let's look at these final two products: the TV-1 and TV-2

Technical Standards Profile (TV-1)

The template[77] for the TV-1 (shown in Figure 2-53) refers to the Joint Technical Architecture (JTA), which has been subsumed by the DoD Information Technology (IT) Standards Registry (DISR) On-line. The DISR On-line provides up-to-date commercial and military standards for use in architecture development. A TV-1 can be generated with this web-based tool on either NIPRnet or SIPRnet. Since these networks are only accessible from a ".mil" address, it makes using such information

_____

[77] DoD Architecture Framework v. 1.0, 9 February 2004, Volume II, p. 6-2

Handwritten margin note: yes, but what's in the DISR?

difficult for contractors. It also means that you will not be able to link this information to your architecture database elements, thus reducing traceability to the architecture elements.

Table 6-1. Technical Standards Profile (TV-1) Template		
JTA Service Area	Service	JTA Standard and Source Document
Information-Processing Standards	Higher Order Languages	
	Software Life-Cycle Process	
	Geospatial Data Interchange	
	Motion Imagery Data Interchange - Video	
	Distributed-Object Computing	
Information-Transfer Standards	Data Flow Network	
	Command and Control Information (C2I) Network	
	Physical Layer	
	Network Interface	
	Layer Management	
	File Transfer Standards	
	Remote Terminal Standards	
	Network Time Synchronization Standards	
	Web Services Standards	
	Connectionless Data Transfer	
	Transport Services Standards	
Information Modeling, Metadata, and Information Exchange Standards	Activity Modeling	
	Data Modeling	
	Object-Oriented Modeling	
Human Computer Interface	Mandates	
Information Security / Information Infrastructure Standards	Password Security	
	Application Software Entity Security Standards	
	Virtual Private Network Service	
	Intrusion Detection Service	
	Human-Computer Interface Security Standards	

Figure 2-53. Missing links to operational and systems elements?

The DoDAF solution for the lack of traceability is to create another matrix (sometimes called the SV-TV Bridge) that uses the TV-1 as the first 3 columns and then adds element IDs for each of the relevant SVs (SV-1/2, SV-4, SV-6 & OV-7/SV-11).[78] We think it's better to capture the relevant standards as part of you architecture database and link them directly to the elements, thus maintaining traceability. You can also extend it to include the operational standards and elements. So use the DISR On-line to generate the list, but include that information in your database.

Figure 2-54 shows an example of a completed TV-1.[79] Note that the standard is only listed using a reference number. That may not be overly helpful to architects who need to understand the impact of the standard on operations and systems. Consider including the relevant information about the standard, any tailoring you need to do to use it in your database, and make sure you include a column with the elements it is associated with. It will reduce the guesswork.

---

[78] See DoD Architecture Framework v. 1.0, 9 February 2004, Volume II, p. 6-4 for this matrix.

[79] DoD Architecture Framework v. 1.0, 9 February 2004, Deskbook, p. 3-50

Service Area	Service	Standard
Operating System	Kernel	FIPS Pub 151-1 (POSIX.1)
	Shell and Utilities	IEEE P1003.2
Software Engineering Services	Programming Languages	FIPS Pub 119 (ADA)
User Interface	Client Server Operations	FIPS Pub 158 (X-Window System)
	Object Definition and Management	DoD Human Computer Interface Style Guide
	Window Management	FIPS Pub 158 (X-Window System)
	Dialogue Support	Project Standard
Data Management	Data Management	FIPS Pub 127-2 (SQL)
Data Interchange	Data Interchange	FIPS Pub 152 (SGML)
	Electronic Data Interchange	FIPS Pub 161 (EDI)
Graphics	Graphics	FIPS Pub 153 (PHIGS)
• • •		

Figure 3.5-6. Notional TV-1

Figure 2-54. Limited information.

Technical Standards Forecast (TV-2)

The last product in the Framework is the TV-2, which provides a future look at the standards that may impact the architecture over its timeframe. No template has been provided, as the DoDAF suggests you simply use the same form as the TV-1, just identify the different timeframes, as appropriate.

You may want to use a variation of TV-1 shown in Figure 2-55.[80] This matrix shows the different time periods when the standards may come into effect. We also suggest that you link this information to the SV-8 and SV-9. By including it in those products, and thus in the Transition Plan, you will create a robust technology roadmap for technology insertion (or as we used to call it – pre-planned product improvement – P3I).

Stuff for a transition plan: SV-8, SV-9, TV-2

(P3I ⇒ incremental development?)

↳ and, I think, you could tailor SV-7 to provide useful insights

---

[80] DoD Architecture Framework v. 1.0, 9 February 2004, Volume II, p. 6-5

Table 6-3. TV-1 Template for Systems with Corresponding Time Periods

Standards Applicable to SV-1 Systems			System A	System B	System C
JTA Service	Service Area	Standard			
Information- Technology Standards	Operating Environment	The DII COE as mandated by the JTA	Current Baseline: Jan. 12, 2003		
	Operating System Standard	ISO/IEC 9945-1:1996, Information Technology - Portable Operating System Interface (POSIX) - Part 1: System Application Program Interface (API) [C language] (Mandated Services). (JTA v2.0/3.1/4.0) http://webstore.ansi.org/ansidocstore/default.asp		Current Baseline: Jan. 12, 2003	Current Baseline: Jan. 12, 2003
	Operating System Standard	ISO/IEC 9945-1:1996:(Thread Extensions) to ISO/IEC 9945-1:1996, Information Technology - Portable Operating System Interface (POSIX) - Part 1: System Application Program Interface (API) [C language] (Thread Optional Services). (JTA v2.0/3.1/4.0) http://webstore.ansi.org/ansidocstore/default.asp	6 months from Baseline	6 months from Baseline	
	Operating System Standard	IEEE 1003.2d:1994, POSIX - Part 2: Shell and Utilities - Amendment: Batch Environment. (JTA v2.0/3.1/4.0) http://standards.ieee.org/catalog/olis/search.html	12 months from Baseline	12 months from Baseline	
	Operating System Standard	Win32 APIs, Window Management and Graphics Device Interface, Volume 1 Microsoft Win32 Programmers Reference Manual, 1993 or later, Microsoft Press. (JTA v2.0/3.1) http://msdn.microsoft.com/default.asp			6 months from Baseline
	Operating System Standard	Win32 APIs, as specified in the Microsoft Platform Software Development Kit (SDK). (JTA v4.0) http://msdn.microsoft.c om/library/default.asp			12 months from Baseline

Figure 2-55. Could be used for the TV-2.

2.2.7 Chapter 2 Summary

In summary, the architecture products represented by the Framework form a set of diagrams that represent some parts, but not all of the architecture. They are linked together through the CADM, but if you don't have a database tool that does this linking for you, you run the risk of creating products that do not tie well together.

That leads us to our second myth, shown below.

Core Architecture Data Model

> **Myth #2: An architecture can be developed in one view only**
>
> ♦ *In reality, the views are just that, views of an architecture and hence are not that easily separable*
>
> ♦ *You may get away with it when trying to document existing architectures, but it guarantees that each view will be sub-optimized*
>
> ♦ Ideally, they should be worked on simultaneously by the same group of people

Many DoD organizations have tried to separate the various views into different architectures, done by different people. We've seen the result and it lacks the true integrated behavior needed for a workable architecture. As this guidance flows down to system developers, they will hopefully pickup the disconnects (hopefully), but it will save the Government significant funds if those errors are detected during the architecture phase. In fact, it's very likely that errors in the architecture phase won't get picked up until test and evaluation or worse during operations, since that's the only time the entire architecture comes back together. Consider this myth carefully in developing your next architecture.

Now that we have introduced the DoDAF products, let's see how it's being applied throughout the DoD and other agencies.

3

How Is DoDAF Being Implemented?

To understand the answer to this question, we need to first look at where these policies derive their authority. The authority comes from Congressional legislation. The table[1] below shows some of the legislative mandates for Information Technology (IT) planning.

Laws and Regulations	Reason the Law or Regulation was Created
Government Performance and Results Act of 1993	- Inadequate program and project evaluation procedures and processes - Inefficient program and project forecasting and planning - Ineffective use of performance metrics - Failure to achieve organizational objectives
Clinger-Cohen Act of 1996	- Uncontrolled capital planning and investment in information systems and IT planning due to the lack of an enterprise architecture - Poor enterprise architecture due to a lack of risk-based security planning throughout the development life cycle
OMB Circular A-11, revised, "Preparation, Submission and Execution of the Budget"	- To establish and organize the budget requirements and process - Provide execution guidelines

OMB Circular A-123, revised, "Management Accountability and Control"	- To address:
	  - Organizational internal control weaknesses
	  - Organizational financial planning and operations inefficiencies
	  - Program and project planning and financial inefficiencies
	  - Financial management and performance risks

OMB Circular A-130, "Management of Federal Information Resources"	- Inadequate security of Government information - Uncontrolled capital planning and investment in information systems and information planning - Systems security breaches - Compromised financial data integrity

The GPRA of 1993 (first on the list) started the whole drive. It recognized the rapidly changing world of IT. Before the early-1980's, DoD tended to drive the technology. Computer systems and software were "mainframe" oriented, thus the big spenders in the Federal Government tended to dictate the pace of technology. But with the introduction of personal computers, all of a sudden the buying power of the entire nation came into the computer market. With that level of interest, entrepreneurs like Bill Gates and Steve Jobs, and large

---

[1] Personal communication from Mr. David Richie's briefing entitled "IT Planning Overview, " December 18, 2003

companies like INTEL and Hewlett-Packard created new products and services at a very rapid pace. New computer generations went from many years to a matter of months. The opening of the Internet in the 1990s accelerated the pace driving the market into a worldwide phenomenon. The impact on the Federal Government was tremendous. No one knew when to invest in this new technology, since it changed so rapidly. The procurement systems were so slow hardware and software would often be obsolete by the time they were received.[2]

In response to these changes, Congress passed GPRA, but it wasn't enough. At roughly the same time, the idea of architectures began to take hold and they were touted to help solve the technology investment problem, along with business process reengineering and other enterprise-wide issues. As a result, the 1996 Clinger-Cohen Act was passed, which required all Administrative Departments create and use enterprise architectures for capital planning and investment.

To implement these laws, the Office of Management and Budget (OMB) issued a number of "circulars" which provided direction of the Departments, including DoD, so they could comply with these new laws. DoD already had their Framework being developed, so they just made sure the products from the Framework mapped to the OMB requirements. Figure 3-1 shows the mapping of the OMB reporting requirements to the Framework products.[3] These circulars are available on the OMB website (http://www.whitehouse.gov/omb/circulars/).

As part of their efforts to bring the entire Administration into compliance with the current laws, the OMB is developing a Federal Enterprise Architecture, which establishes reference models (RM) for use in developing enterprise architectures.[4] Figure 3-2 shows these reference models and their status as of February 2006. They have been pulled together into a *Consolidated Reference Model* (CRM).[5] The Data Reference Model (DRM) was updated more recently and should help improve the sharing of information between Federal Government organizations, if applied correctly.

The information provided in these reference models defines common terms for business processes, services, performance, and data. However, DoD has established those terms and architecture products; hence, a mapping between the DoD policies and approach was necessary. As

---

[2] In the mid-1980's the Air Force made a large-scale procurement for personal computers that were nearly obsolete by the time they were received and distributed.

[3] DoD Architecture Framework 1.0, 9 February 2004, Volume I, p. 2-2

[4] These reference models can be found at http://www.whitehouse.gov/omb/egov/a-1-fea.html.

[5] FY07 Budget Formulation, FEA Consolidated Reference Model Document, Executive Office of the President of the United States, May 2005

such, OSD is developing reference models that mirror the FEA RMs. The DoD RMs are available at http://www.dod.mil/nii/ea/.

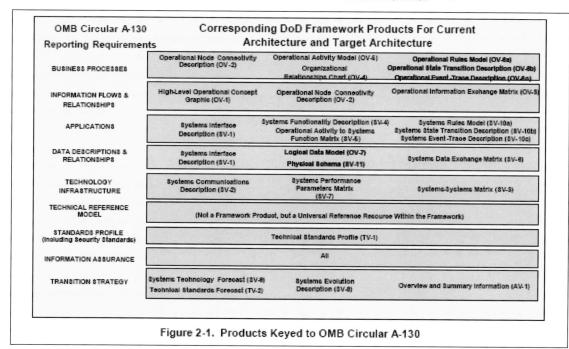

Figure 2-1. Products Keyed to OMB Circular A-130

Figure 3-1. DoDAF products map well to OMB requirements.

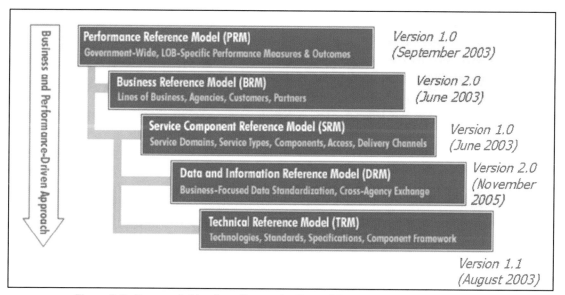

Figure 3-2. Now available altogether as the Consolidated Reference Model (CRM).

DoD Architecture Framework

Figure 3-3 shows this type of mapping and the relationship to the Global Information Grid architecture.[6] Figure 3-4 takes the RMs one more level and shows how to map them to the DoDAF products. Hence, you can trace from the FEA RMs to the DoDAF products by following these diagrams.

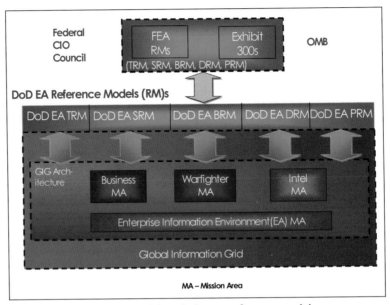

Figure 3-3. DoD has their own reference models.

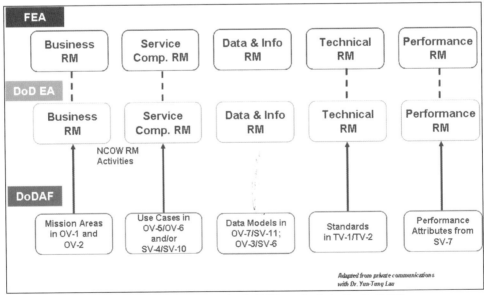

Figure 3-4. We can map the DoDAF products to the DoD RMs.

---

[6] DoD Enterprise Architecture Executive Summary, v0.04, August 20, 2005, DoD EA Congruence Community of Practice, p. 2

With this background, let's now look at the key documents that reference the DoDAF. Some of the key documents include:

- DoD Directive 5000.1, "The Defense Acquisition System," May 12, 2003
- DoD Instruction 5000.2, "Operation of the Defense Acquisition System," May 12, 2003
- CJCSI 3170.01E, "Joint Capabilities Integration and Development System (JCIDS)," dated 11 May 2005
- DoD Directive 4630.5, "Interoperability and Supportability of Information Technology (IT) and National Security Systems (NSS)," dated May 5, 2004 [see DoDI 4630.8 and CJCSI 6212.01C for more details]
- "Levels of Information Systems Interoperability (LISI)," dated March 30, 1998.

We will discuss each of these at a high level. For more details, you can obtain all these documents on the web. The DoD directives and instructions can be found at http://www.dtic.mil/whs/directives. The CJCS instructions can be obtained from http://www.dtic.mil/cjcs_directives.[7]

3.1 The DoD Decision Support System Framework

The DoD Decision Support System (shown in Figure 3-5) combines the Defense Acquisition System (The 5000 Series, which replaces the Acquisition Management System) with the Planning, Programming, Budgeting, and Execution cycle (which replaced the Planning, Programming and Budgeting System – PPBS), with the Joint Capabilities Integration and Development System (JCIDS, which replaces the Requirements Generation System). These three policies form the new way DoD management is determining what systems to obtain to enhance our warfighting and other DoD mission capabilities.

The 5000 series documents the way DoD acquires new capabilities and systems. This series of documents have been revised over the years, but a major revision occurred in 2003, just prior to the publication of the DoDAF. The purpose of the 5000 series is "to acquire quality products that satisfy user needs with measurable improvements to mission capability and operational support, in a timely manner, and at a fair and reasonable price."[8] The policy recognizes the need for flexibility, responsiveness, innovation, discipline, and streamlined effective management.

---

[7] Please note that all URLs provided are as of February 2006. Since these often change you may have to search for this information.

[8] DoD Directive 5000.1, United States of America Department of Defense, May 12, 2003, p. 2

The 5000 series also describes the acquisition lifecycle, its major milestones and responsibilities of the various DoD organizations. It also requires all financial and "mixed" information systems to be compliant with the Financial Management Enterprise Architecture (FMEA – now the Business Enterprise Architecture).

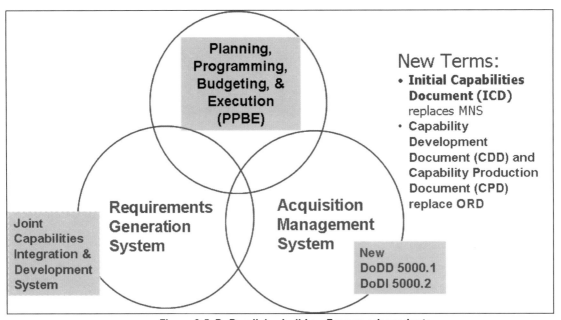

Figure 3-5. DoD policies build on Framework products.

The PPBE replaced the Planning, Programming, and Budgeting System (PPBS) in 2003, as part of the Defense Planning Guidance (DPG) that streamlined the DoD decision-making and budgeting process. PPBE uses a "two-year budget cycle, which allows DoD to formulate two-year budgets and use the Off-Budget year to focus on budget execution and evaluate program performance."[9]

The PPBE continually changes each year, with the current and upcoming budget execution years, as well as the Future Years Defense Program (FYDP) that looks ahead 6 additional years. Hence, the planning cycle is 8 years. That's potentially 8 -10 computer generations. The need for technology insertion and projection becomes critical if we intend to keep our capabilities in line with the technology.

More information on the PPBE is available from handbooks and other documents on the Defense Acquisition University website.[10]

---

[9] From http://www.dod.mil/comptroller/icenter/budget/histcontext.htm, obtained from that website on February 26, 2006.

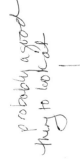

[10] For example, see Manager's Guide to Technology Transition in an Evolutionary Acquisition Environment (2005), available at
http://www.dau.mil/pubs/guidebook/managers_guide.asp

The last document of the decision support framework is JCIDS. Let's now discuss that document in a bit more detail, as it is the lynchpin for this new approach to acquisition.

3.2 Joint Capabilities Integration and Development System (JCIDS)

Perhaps one of the most interesting documents in this decision framework is the Joint Capabilities Integration & Development System (JCIDS).[11] JCIDS defines the policies and procedures for obtaining Warfighter needs and describes the oversight structure, roles, and responsibilities. It also defines the various documents that the architect must produce throughout the 5000 lifecycle. Figure 3-6[12] shows the overlay of the document deliveries and approval by the Joint Requirements Oversight Council (JROC) in advance of major lifecycle milestones.

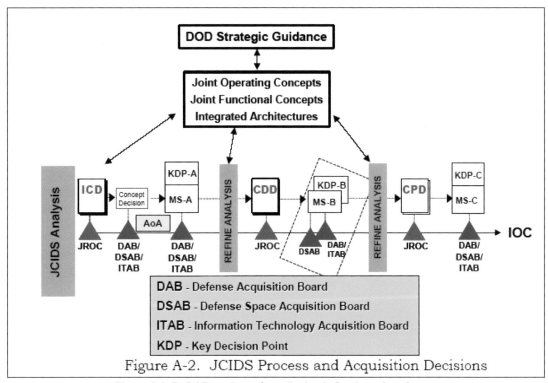

Figure A-2. JCIDS Process and Acquisition Decisions

Figure 3-6. DoDAF products form the basis for these key documents.

These documents require the delivery of specific architecture products. The Initial Capabilities Document (ICD, not to be confused with the Interface Control Document, which always used this acronym before) requires only the OV-1. The Capabilities Development Document

---

[11] The latest version of this document is CJCSI 3170.01E, Joint Capabilities Integration & Development System, 11 May 2005

[12] CJCSI 3170.01E, Joint Capabilities Integration & Development System, 11 May 2005, p. A-8

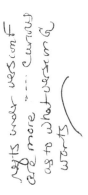

(CDD) requires the OV-1, OV-2, OV-3, OV-5, SV-1/SV-2, and SV-6. The Capabilities Production Document (CPD) requires the OV-1, OV-2, OV-3, OV-5, OV-6c, SV-1/SV-2, SV-6, and TV-1, with the OV-6b and SV-10b as optional products. The ICD replaces the Mission Needs Statement (MNS) and the combination of the CDD and CPD replace the Operational Requirements Document (ORD). The Capstone Requirements Document (CRD) has been replaced by a combination of the ICD and the Joint Capabilities Document (JCD). Clearly, the DoDAF products have become a major factor in the acquisition of new defense systems.

JCIDS also defines a process for the identifying the capability needs of the DoD (see Figure 3-7[13]). This "top-down" approach starts with the National Security Strategy (NSS) and works its way down through the integrated architecture (defined by DoDAF products) to identify needed capabilities and any changes in the force structure.

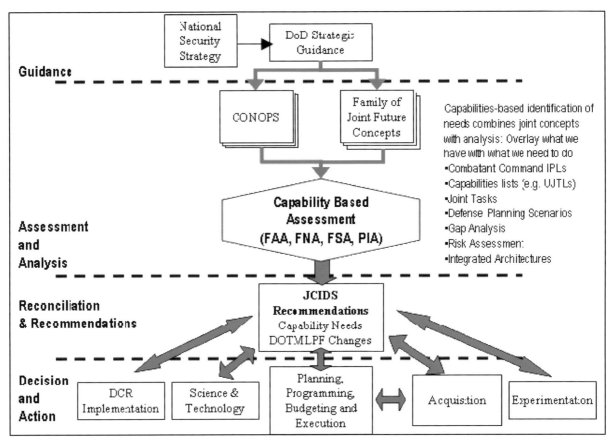

Figure 3-7. Top Down Capability Need Identification Process.

The JCIDS capability based assessment consists of four analyses: 1) Functional Area Analysis (FAA); 2) Functional Needs Analysis (FNA); 3)

---

[13] CJCSI 3170.01E, Joint Capabilities Integration & Development System, 11 May 2005, p. A-4

Functional Solutions Analysis (FSA); and 4) Post Independent Analysis (PIA).

FAA (another overloaded acronym) "identifies the operational tasks, conditions and standards needed to achieve military objectives."[14] This analysis develops the scenarios for use in assessing the capabilities of the architecture.

The FNA "assesses the ability of the current and programmed warfighting systems to deliver the capabilities the FAA identified under the full range of operating conditions and to the designated measures of effectiveness."[15] This analysis defines the capability needs for the doctrine, organization, training, materiel, leadership and education, personnel, facilities, (DOTMLPF) and policy affected by the architecture. In this process, the analyst identifies the capability gaps.

The FSA provides potential solutions to resolve the capability gaps. It documents the gaps, these alternative solutions and the integrated architectures that link them to existing systems. This analysis should also identify excess capabilities or unnecessarily redundant systems for potential elimination.[16]

The PIA uses an independent group to conduct a review of the FSA to "ensure it was thorough and that the recommended non-materiel and materiel approaches are reasonable possibilities to deliver the capability identified in the FAA and/or FNA."[17] The results of this review are used in the analysis of alternatives (AoA), which starts the process of developing an ICD.

Clearly this process is a little bit of a "chicken and egg." You need an architecture to perform these analyses (in fact all the steps in these analyses are part of the architecture development approach I recommend), yet it appears that these analyses are needed to start the process of developing an architecture. In fact, what this really means is you need to look at the architecture development process as a series of analyses at more and more detailed levels of decomposition. Hence, in these JCIDS analyses, you need to create a high level architecture, with the result being reported with an ICD. Each of the subsequent documents (CDD & CPD) need to refine the architecture by continuing the analysis in greater depth, *until you have defined the top level*

---

[14] CJCSI 3170.01E, Joint Capabilities Integration & Development System, 11 May 2005, p. A-4

[15] CJCSI 3170.01E, Joint Capabilities Integration & Development System, 11 May 2005, p. A-5

[16] Although we know that it is very difficult to get rid of old systems. They always have advocates. It took the Year 2000 (Y2K) for us to get rid of a lot of these ancient "pet rocks."

[17] CJCSI 3170.01E, Joint Capabilities Integration & Development System, 11 May 2005, p. A-5

requirements of the systems you need to develop to implement the capabilities defined in these analyses. Hence, the end result of the architecture is to create a series of solid requirements documents for system developer. Then the classical system engineering process takes over.

What we've seen happen, is these "analyses" often come from a "BOGSAT" (bunch of guys and gals sitting around a table). The "experts" or "representatives" of organizations get together and decide what the gaps are (because they know and no analysis is really necessary) and what the new performance parameters ought to be. In case you think I'm making this up, I give you an example. In a recent project I worked on (which shall remain nameless), I was trying to understand where the performance numbers embedded in an ICD came from. I found out that an employee of one of our FFRDCs[18] was given a few days to come up with the performance numbers. He guessed what they should be from his experience, which was good, but it defeats the intent of having hard analysis drive this process. I don't believe this is an isolated incident. It has been common practice for as long as I've been involved in DoD projects. The timelines get artificially set and this becomes the result. Fortunately, we caught the problem and have begun to work on a more analytical basis for the performance metrics. However, this is the kind of problem JCIDS was supposed to help fix. It's a step in the right direction, but we're "not there yet."

We will come back to another important part of JCIDS in Section 3.4, but before we do, let's discuss a couple of other key requirements documents: CJCSI 6212.01C and the LISI.

3.3 DoD's Requirements for Interoperability: CJCSI 6212.01C and LISI

Since interoperability was a key driver for all these new policy changes, the policy for interoperability was one of the first to adopt emerging standards. CJCSI 6212.01C, *Interoperability and Supportability of National Security Systems, and Information Technology Systems*, was "published" on November 20, 2003. It aligns with JCIDS and the Net-Centric Operations and Warfare (NCOW) Reference Model. It also details a methodology to develop net-ready key performance parameters (NR-KPP) and defines the Information Support Plan (ISP), which replaces the C4ISP of pervious versions, thus extending it beyond the C4ISR domain. CJCSI 6212 is referenced in a number of other documents including: CJCSI 3170.01E, DoDD 4630.5, DoDI 4630.8, and DoDD 8100.1. It also describes the policies and procedures for Joint Interoperability Test Command (JITC), the system interoperability test certification, and ISP certification, which will discuss more in Section 3.4.

---

[18] Federally Funded Research and Development Center

The NR-KPP consists of measurable and testable characteristics, including performance metrics. These metrics determine how well the architecture will satisfy information needs for a given capability, and include timeliness, accuracy, and information assurance. It states: "All elements of the NR-KPP will be able to be measured, tested or evaluated."[19] However, this document also states that the NR-KPP will include compliance with the NCOW Reference Model, compliance with GIG Key Interface Profiles[20] (KIP) and supporting architecture products. As a result, this simple metric includes a rather substantial document trail.

Figure 3-8[21] shows the DoDAF products associated with the Net-Ready KPP and how they relate to the other documents needed in the JCIDS process. This figure also includes a document we haven't discussed: the ISP or Information Support Plan.

Document	Net-Ready Key Performance Parameter Products																	
	Supporting Architecture Products														NCOW RM	KIP Compliance	IA Compliance	LISI Profile
	AV-1	OV-1	OV-2	OV-3	OV-4	OV-5	OV-6C	SV-1	SV-2	SV-3	SV-4	SV-5	SV-6	TV-1				
ICD		X													X			
CDD	X		X		X	X	X				X	X	X	X	X	X	X	X Basic
CPD	X		X		X	X	X				X	X	X	X	X	X	X	X Complete
CRD		X		1		2									2	2	2	
ISP	3	3	3		3	3	3	3			3	3	3	3	3	3	3	3 Complete

Note: X = Required
   (1) Old CRDs Updates
   (2) New CRDs
   (3) ACAT, NON ACAT and Fielded Systems. NR-KPP products produced for the CDD and CPD will be used in the ISP.

Table A-2. JCIDS Documents/NR-KPP Products Matrix.

Figure 3-8. NR-KPPs require architecture products.

CJCSI 6212 provides an outline of the ISP, as shown in Figure 3-9. The architecture products, which form part of the analysis section,

---

[19] CJCI 6212.01C, Interoperability and Supportability of National Security Systems, and Information Technology Systems, November 20, 2003, p. A-6

[20] The KIP contains a lot of information, including refined operational and systems view products, interface control documents and specifications, engineering management plan, configuration management plan, TV-1 with SV-TV bridge, and procedures for standards conformance and interoperability testing. Another large documentation set.

[21] CJCI 6212.01C, Interoperability and Supportability of National Security Systems, and Information Technology Systems, November 20, 2003, p. A-6

include DoDAF products and other documents. In addition, it requires a SV-6 matrix in Microsoft Excel format for assessment during the certification process.

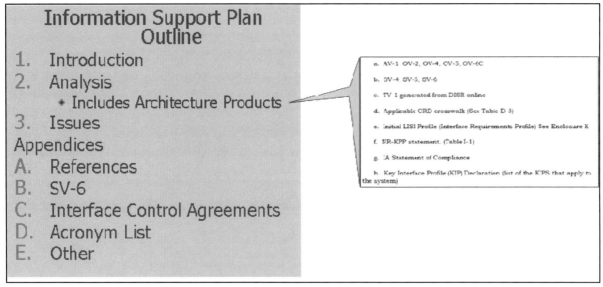

Figure 3-9. The ISP requires architecture products as well.

Note also that the ISP is designed "to document the IT and NSS needs, objectives, interface requirements for all non-ACAT and fielded programs." As a result, the ISP must be produced for all programs, no matter what their development status, *which means we must provide architecture products for everything out there* or at least recognize some of our existing documentation as containing the information needed to create the architecture products.

Another architecture product mentioned in CJCSI 6212 is the "LISI profile." Let's look at what LISI is all about.

Levels of Information System Interoperability (LISI)

LISI was developed concurrently with the C4ISR Architecture Framework and was originally included as Appendix D to that document (dated 23 September 1997). It was released as a stand-alone document by the C4ISR Architecture Working Group (AWG) on 30 March 1998. LISI was cast as a process maturity model. It defines the 5 levels of interoperability to determine maturity of a system or architecture. Figure 3-10 shows the levels and their meaning.[22] It assumes that we want all systems to move toward the "Enterprise" level, making them interoperable with whoever needs them, wherever needed. Although the goal meets the definition of "net-centric," you may discover that there are times that "isolated" is the preferred level of interoperability. For

---

[22] "Levels of Information System Interoperability," released by the C4ISR Architecture Working Group, March 30, 1998, p. ES-4

example, if you have a Special Operations Force platoon on an operation, they may not want to be contacted. But of course, there will be times they want contact as well, so you can see that interoperability may be a situation-dependent quantity.

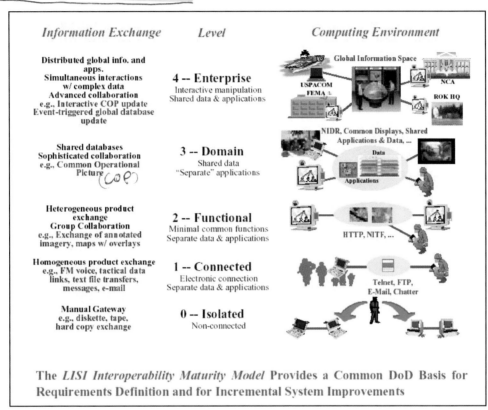

Figure 3-10. LISI helps define what we mean by "interoperable."

LISI also introduces its own framework for describing architectures: the **PAID** Model. PAID stands for procedures, applications, infrastructure, and data (see Figure 3-11)[23]. *Procedures* are documented guidance, such as standards and policies, and operational "controls" (e.g., standard operating procedures) that affect the development, integration and operation of the architecture. *Applications* include its mission, functional requirements, and means of accomplishing those functions, which we would take as software applications or services. *Infrastructure* refers to the "connections" between systems or applications, including networks, hardware, and security equipment. *Data* describes the information processed by the architecture and includes both the format and meaning of the data elements.

---

[23] "Levels of Information System Interoperability," released by the C4ISR Architecture Working Group, March 30, 1998, p. 2-9

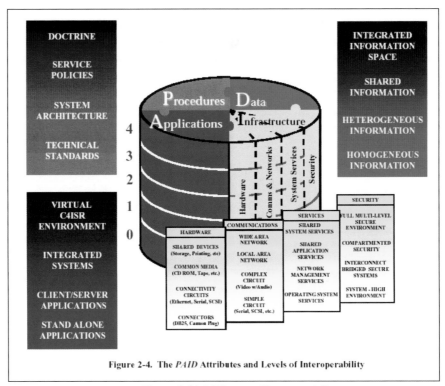

Figure 2-4. The *PAID* Attributes and Levels of Interoperability

Figure 3-11. LISI's own "framework."

LISI relates the PAID model to the maturity levels in Figure 3-12 using the LISI reference model.[24]

Description	Computing Environment	Level	**P**	**A**	**I**	**D**
Enterprise	Universal	4	Enterprise Level	Interactive	Multi-Dimensional Topologies	Enterprise Model
Domain	Integrated	3	Domain Level	Groupware	World-wide Networks	Domain Model
Functional	Distributed	2	Program Level	Desktop Automation	Local Networks	Program Model
Connected	Peer-to-Peer	1	Local/Site Level	Standard System Drivers	Simple Connection	Local
Isolated	Manual	0	Access Control	N/A	Independent	Private

Figure 3-1. LISI Reference Model

Figure 3-12. LISI relates the PAID model to the maturity levels.

---

[24] "Levels of Information System Interoperability," released by the C4ISR Architecture Working Group, March 30, 1998, p. 3-2

Translating the information required in the PAID model from the DoDAF may not be obvious, but clearly both PAID and DoDAF attempt to describe architectures, hence given a complete architecture, we should be able to develop products that can be evaluated by either one.

LISI provides a process and tool (see Figure 3-13[25]) that aids you in determining the state of your architecture's interoperability. The tool is the LISI Interoperability Questionnaire that asks detailed questions about your systems. You may find this difficult for the "To-Be" architecture, but very helpful for an "As-Is," which is where you would really want this assessment anyway and to see where you could have possible interoperability problems. The resulting profile (yes, this is the LISI profile mentioned in CJCSI 6212) maps the data obtained from the questionnaire to the capability model. The information is captured in a repository where you can produce other products like the S2 interoperability matrix, which you may recognize as a form of the SV-3. You can also overlay the information on a nodal diagram, which would be the SV-1 or SV-2. Thus, you can use the DoDAF products and LISI *to demonstrate interoperability or where you have gaps in interoperability.* The end result is a powerful presentation for decision makers.

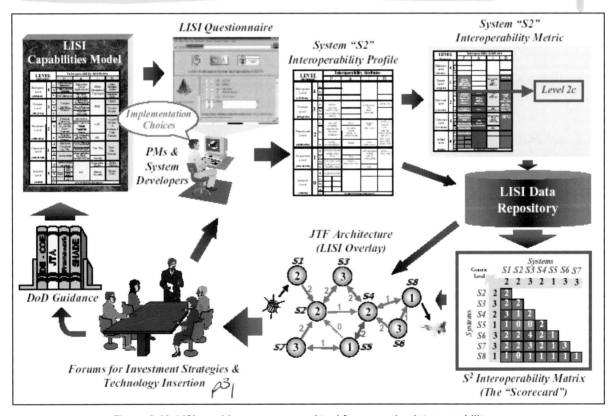

Figure 3-13. LISI provides a process and tool for assessing interoperability.

25 "Levels of Information System Interoperability," released by the C4ISR Architecture Working Group, March 30, 1998, p. 4-1

Since I've brought up decision making, why don't we talk about how the architectures get evaluated?

3.4 How Will Architectures Be Evaluated?

Before we get into the process for evaluation, let's discuss the role of the architect in development process in DoD. Architects provide vision, techniques, tools and processes to develop the architecture. They also must take responsibility for the results, and hence, they must have a Government (DoD) sponsor. They also must make the results understandable to a wide audience, including decision-makers, warfighters and other architects, because we know all these groups of people will have something to say about the architecture. Perhaps the most important item of concern is the architect must deal with the politics of the architecture and DoD; and like any other large institution or business, it has a lot of politics. Since architecture is being used to determine who gets money and who doesn't (aside from the usual Congressional earmarks), the architect has to be someone who can represent the DoD in the evaluation and approval process, which can include the Congress, OMB, GAO, and other organizations within the Federal Government. So, the bottom line is that the real architect for a DoD architecture must be a government representative, which usually means a government employee.

Many government employees don't realize this when they've been tapped to be the government Program Manager for an architecture project. They think they can hire a contractor and then stand back and let the contractor do all the work. They will find that's a quick way to be demoted (even if they can't be fired, there's always assignments available in some awful part of the world). I've seen it happen, particularly on high profile projects. So be warned. If you are a contractor, please make sure your government lead understands this and provide them with all the support they need to be successful.

Evaluation occurs during the architecture design process and during the approval phase. Since the Framework does not tell you how to build architectures, only what products/data are needed for evaluation, you have to develop a methodology for developing the architecture. I have found that you will need to apply proven system engineering processes to be successful. When using them, make sure you document the methodology and any tailoring of techniques (as discussed in Chapter 2). You also should attack the problem holistically, not by passing out views for people to build independently. I have seen this done in a number of architecture projects, only to see a major struggle to integrate the products at the end. You also should map your architecture to higher-level architectures, such as the GIG and FMEA/BEA.

During the approval phase, critical Independent Verification and Validation (IV&V) comes from ASD/NII and MITRE personnel. Be aware of what evaluation criteria, they use and make sure you provide any extra documentation, beyond Framework products, needed to communicate architecture results. Again, make sure that the methodology selected and any tailoring applied is communicated. I like to include a methodology appendix to the AV-1. For all architectures that require funding in DoD, JCIDS defines a set of architecture governance boards as shown in Figure 3-14.[26]

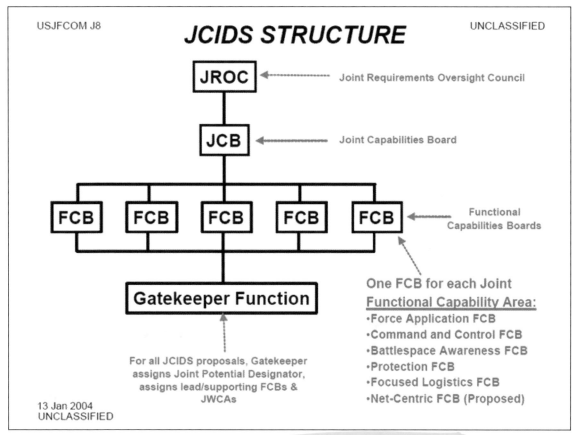

Figure 3-14. **JCIDS defines the governance structure for DoD.**

The Gatekeeper function (run by an O-7!) filters the proposals and make sure they are ready for the next level of review: the functional capabilities boards (FCB). The FCBs are divided into different domains; hence, your architectures will likely be reviewed by multiple boards, which will be looking for things in their area of expertise. The joint capabilities board then makes sure an integrated result is forwarded to the JROC for final approval. As you can imagine, a process with this many levels of review won't be fast and you will have to make sure that the staff at each level have the information they need to properly evaluate the architecture products. So, we can see how architectures will be

[26] Presented by Ms. Kim Frisby, USJFCOM/J89 at the DoD Architectures Conference February 25, 2004

evaluated prior to design and development. But how do architectures play in the real evaluation of the resulting systems? Let's take a look.

Interoperability and Supportability Certification, Testing, and Validation

CJCSI 6212 defines the processes for interoperability and supportability testing. J-6 (Joint Chiefs of Staff Directorate for C4 Systems) will validate that you have obtained or developed the capabilities interoperability and supportability certification, JITC Joint System Interoperability Test Certification, and the NR-KPP. This document also defines the processes for JCIDS acquisition category (ACAT) programs, non-ACAT and fielded capabilities (in other words everything). The processes for each are shown in Figure 3-15,[27] 3-16,[28] and 3-17[29]. The ACAT programs have interoperability certifications occurring prior to the CDD and CPD developments. Note also that the ISP gets delivered twice in this process.

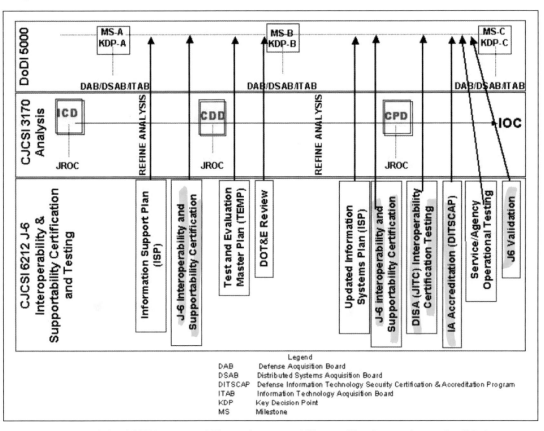

Figure 3-15. ACAT interoperability and supportability certification testing and validation.

[27] CJCI 6212.01C, Interoperability and Supportability of National Security Systems, and Information Technology Systems, November 20, 2003, p. A-10

[28] CJCI 6212.01C, Interoperability and Supportability of National Security Systems, and Information Technology Systems, November 20, 2003, p. A-16

[29] CJCI 6212.01C, Interoperability and Supportability of National Security Systems, and Information Technology Systems, November 20, 2003, p. A-19

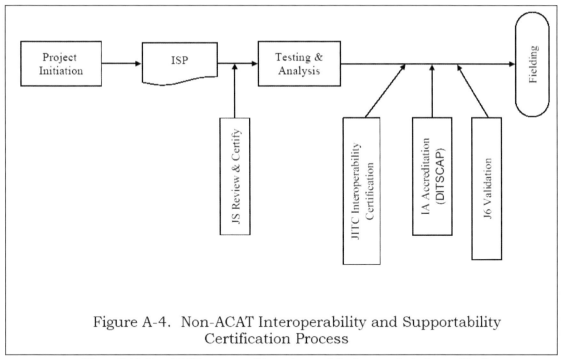

Figure A-4. Non-ACAT Interoperability and Supportability
Certification Process

Figure 3-16. Non-ACAT process still requires architecture products for certification.

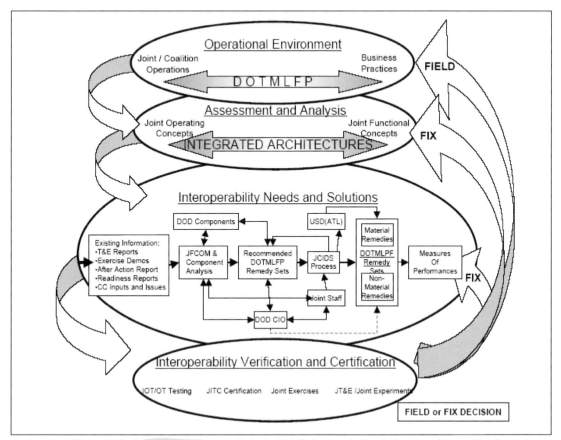

Figure 3-17. Even fielded systems must provide integrated architectures for certification.

The process for the non-ACAT programs is simpler, because it only requires the ISP and JTIC interoperability certification to be provided once, but that still requires a significant amount of work. Even the fielded programs have to deal with the architectures and certification. What's most interesting about this process is they only have "field or fix" options. I hope they will include "phase out" or "cancel" as other options.

Well I've said that the JITC certification is critical to the evaluation process. Let's look at how JITC certifies interoperability and supportability.

JITC Certification Process

The JITC, based in Fort Huachuca, AZ, was tasked by CJCSI 6212 with the responsibility to conduct interoperability and supportability evaluations and testing. Figure 3-18 shows their process for system life-cycle certification.[30] It begins with the JCIDS and other architecture-related documents, which include the NR-KPP. These documents are analyzed to ensure that standards, in particular communications standards, have been met. This analysis occurs from the documents and any data collected during developmental testing. They then attempt to evaluate interoperability in the most operational realistic environment possible, as part of the operational test and evaluation (OT&E), using a representative production sample of the system under test. Certification occurs during these steps.

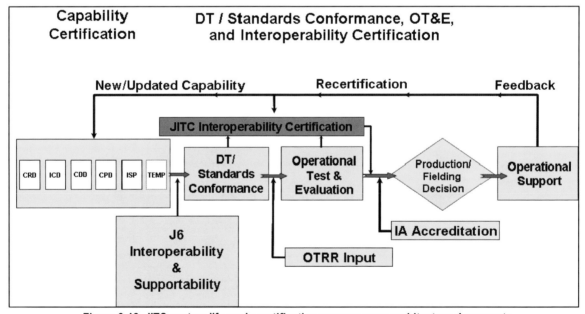

Figure 3-18. JITC system life-cycle certification process uses architecture documents.

---

[30] From a briefing entitled "JITC Interoperability Certification Process," Joint Interoperability Test Command, Plans and Policies Branch, obtained from http://jitc.fhu.disa.mil/testing.htm, March 1, 2006.

The JITC has also developed a web-based interoperability tool (Joint Interoperability Tool – JIT – as seen in Figure 3-19). The website is located at http://jit.fhu.disa.mil/. This website is one of the many evaluation tools DoD is making available to help programs meet the interoperability needs of our net-centric systems. We must not forget that people will be conducting these evaluations, and to make the process easier, we need to know their needs.

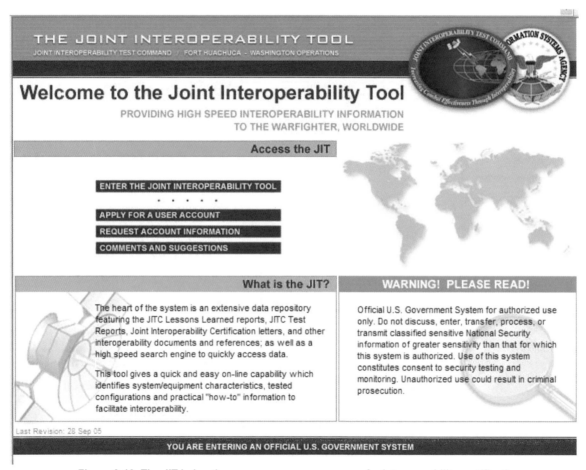

Figure 3-19. The JIT helps the program manager prepare for interoperability certification.

Insights into Architecture Evaluator Needs

Perhaps the most important thing to remember in all this discussion of policies and evaluation is that our job as architects and contractors supporting the architecture development entails understanding how the architectures will be used in the decision making process. Figure 3-20 shows a set of questions that evaluators might ask at all different levels.[31] Please recognize that you will be developing an architecture that may be evaluated at any and all these levels. The more you understand

---

[31] DoD Architecture Framework 1.0, 9 February 2004, Volume I, p. 3-8

93

how the evaluators will want to see and use your architecture, the much better off you will be.

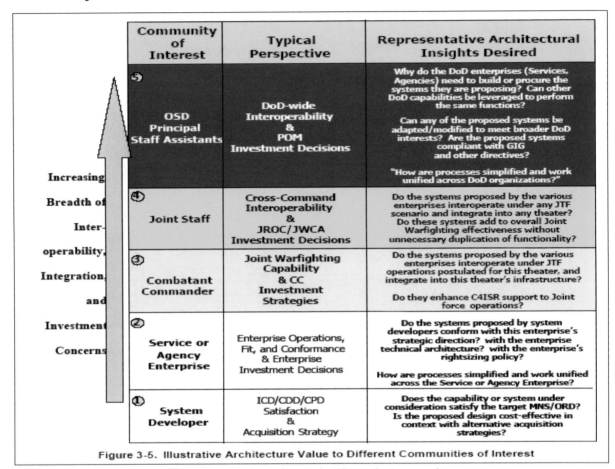

Figure 3-5. Illustrative Architecture Value to Different Communities of Interest

Figure 3-20. It helps to know what the evaluators need.

Up to this point, I've provided a lot of background into what architectures are, what the Framework is, and the policies that guide architecture development. We now need to better understand how to build and communicate the results of your architecture. The rest of this book will discuss how to build executable architectures.

4

What's the DoDAF Missing?

I hope you now have a better understanding of architectures and the DoDAF, as well as their implementation in Federal Government and DoD. But as we have said all the way through, the Framework and policies only define the products or end results of the architecture development. How can we develop the architecture?

Well, the DoDAF provides a six-step process for developing architectures.[1] It is not meant to be a detailed architecture development process, only an overview of what you need to do.

The DoDAF recommends that the process used encompass six steps:

- Step 1: Determine the intended use of the architecture description
- Step 2: Determine the architecture description's scope, context, environment, and any other assumptions to be considered
- Step 3: Based on the intended use and the scope, determine what information the architecture description needs to capture
- Step 4: Determine products to be built
- Step 5: Gather the data and build the requisite products
- Step 6: Use the architecture description for its intended purpose

Note how this implies *if you build the products, then you build the architecture.* I have found from experience that nothing could be further from the truth. What's missing is really buried in Step 5. It's methodology: the techniques, processes, and tools that you use to develop architectures. This leads us to our third myth about the Framework.

Myth #3: The Framework provides a methodology for developing architectures

- ♦ *In reality, no detailed methodology was provided. It provides some guidelines and suggested process steps in Volume I and Deskbook, but there is no detailed methodology that could evaluated using the CMMI or other process standard*
- ♦ *This lack of a methodology was on purpose, to avoid force fitting a methodology on the Commands, Services and Agencies. Instead it was assumed that each of these organizations and their support contractors had effective methodologies in-place*
- ♦ *The Framework only provides a means for comparing architectures by means of these products*

---

[1] DoD Architecture Framework 1.0, 9 February 2004, Volume I, p. 5-4 through 5-6

Let's now discuss what we mean by methodology and how it will help us develop architectures.

Methodology

As the quote in the box says, the DoDAF recognized the need for methodology; however, it's not emphasized in the document. We just assumed everyone would understand that the Framework was designed to be methodology independent. After all, who would expect the Navy to conduct an architectural analysis the same was as the Army?

> *"... the need for a well-defined and rigorous methodology is acknowledged and emphasized."*
> DoD Architecture Framework, Version 1.0 (09 February 2004) Volume II, p. 2-8

So what does the word "methodology" mean? The Webster's II New College Dictionary 2001, defines methodology as: "1) The system of principles, procedures, and practices applied to a particular branch of knowledge; and 2) the branch of logic dealing with the general principles of the formation of knowledge." That definition gives us some idea of what's needed, but I like to put it in more practical terms: techniques, processes and tools.[2] As architects, we need to supply techniques, processes and tools for analyzing user needs and developing a complete, executable model of the architecture. But before we get into the details, what does methodology do for us?

Methodology provides the structure for attacking any problem, in this case the problem of how to develop architectures. If we have the theoretical underpinnings right and a process for implementing the theory, it's then "just" a matter of following the technique and process. Tools act as aids to enforce the rules associated with the theory and process. Hence, you can have a team of people working concurrently on different parts of the problem (e.g., different domains, such as tracked vehicles and C4ISR systems) and have confidence that they can be brought together in a common structure. *Since the DoDAF is methodology independent, we must select our own methodology.*

So where do we go to find methodologies for architecture? Well since the DoDAF is built on a set of system engineering diagrams, let's look at system engineering first.

System Engineering Methodologies for Architectures

System engineering has two aspects to it: a technical orientation and a management orientation. The technical orientation provides a

---

[2] As an aside, we use the mantra "people, processes and tools" to describe the approach to any job in a proposal. The idea of technique instead of process puts methodology in a more theoretical vain than the approach. Obviously you need people as well, but we will leave them out for the time being.

comprehensive, iterative problem-solving process that is used to: 1) transform customer requirements into a solution set; 2) generate information for decision-makers; and 3) provide information for the next phase. The management orientation provides the controls needed to achieve an optimum balance of all system elements in the architecture.

Systems Engineering (SE) focuses on defining customer needs and the required functionality (capabilities) early in the development cycle, encourages the documentation of requirements, and then enables the synthesis of a verifiable design. SE provides an interdisciplinary approach and means to develop successful systems. These disciplines include:

- Operations
- Performance
- Test
- Manufacturing
- Cost & Schedule
- Training & Support
- Disposal

SE integrates all these disciplines and specialty groups into a team effort forming a structured development process that proceeds from concept to production to operation. SE considers both the business and the technical needs of all customers with the goal of providing a quality product that meets the user needs. SE principles include: requirements definition; linkage between all elements of the system; accountability for the results; balance between competing factions; iterative decomposition of requirements, functions and components; measurements and metrics to be able to quantify when you've met the requirements; standards-based control; and optimization to perform the necessary trade-offs between cost, schedule and performance. The proper application of system engineering requires *rigor*, *discipline*, and *consistency*.

So how do we go about doing SE? The principal approaches are decomposition and classification (or categorization – not to be confused with security classification). In decomposition, we break down high-level, abstract elements, such as requirements, functions, and components, into more easily digestible pieces. The reason we do this, because as humans, we can only get our heads wrapped around so much information. We also can only solve simple, linear problems ; the way we solve most non-linear problems is by converting them to linear problems over portions of the non-linear region. There is a danger to decomposition: you can easily lose

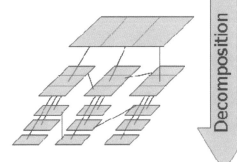

track of your place; and as a result, you can break the linkages between the pieces. Hence, traceability of the decomposition or the decomposition hierarchy becomes very important to be able to use and visualize.

Classification divides information into groups that make things simpler to understand. We do it by looking at the characteristics of the objects we want to classify and assigning them to the groups. In information or data modeling, we call this the "schema" for the capturing of information about the topic. Schema development requires significant domain understanding to avoid duplication of categories, which would result in confusion about which bin to put what object. We inherited the concept of classification from the Greeks[3] and has been used in all varieties of science ever since. Imagine how hard chemistry would be without the periodic table? *The bottom-line is we need to have a methodology that enables us to decompose and classify the complete architecture and its behavior.* Some other factors we need to include from SE are metrics, processes, and standards.

Metrics

Metrics are measurements that help you make a decision or take an action. In other words, you aren't collecting a metric just because it's something you can measure. For metrics to be useful, we need to define the expected performance, decision thresholds, and the maximum range acceptable. Figure 4-1 depicts the kind of metrics graph you might want to develop as a decision aid. The expected performance is shown as a simple line, although it could be a more complex relationship. The thresholds provide a visual transition point so you can take a corrective action. The corrective action for a performance metric would be to look for ways to reduce the size of the rocket payload (it got too big for the launch vehicle). As you get further away from the expected performance, you might have to re-plan the effort. Re-planning seems to be an annual occurrence in most programs I've observed.

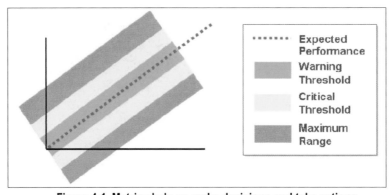

Figure 4-1. Metrics help us make decisions and take actions.

---

[3] Building Enterprise Information Architectures, Melissa A. Cook, 1996, p. 53, Prentice Hall PTR.

Process

A process includes the functions or activities, which transforms inputs to outputs and the sequencing of the functions, activities, or steps. Often, people will focus on the inputs/outputs (OV-5/SV-4) or the functional sequencing (OV-6/SV-10), but you need both to capture the process completely. I've also found it makes a big difference when I consider them together. Figure 4-2 shows a generic process and examples of the kinds of inputs and outputs. The sequencing show is a simple, sequential set of steps (subordinate activities), but most processes are much more complex, particularly when you include failure modes and feedback.

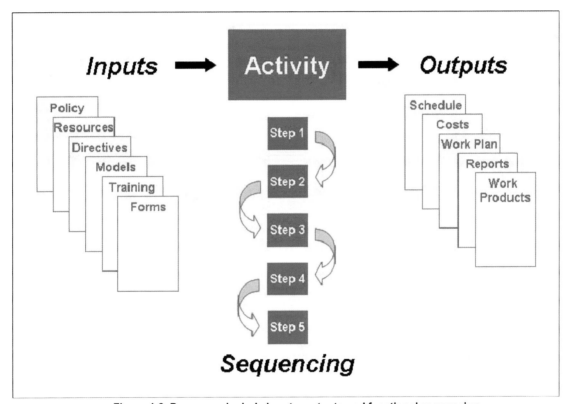

Figure 4-2. Processes include inputs, outputs and functional sequencing.

Each step will have its own subordinate process, with the same rules. I've found many people have difficulty with this concept and want to call each level of process by a different name (activities to steps to base practices, to ...), but they are really all the same thing. Try to avoid this pitfall, it will make your life very complicated and adds confusion to the discussion.

Standards

What is a standard? It is a *document* that establishes engineering and technical requirements for processes, products, and procedures. It's a document, because you need to have it written down and agreed to by everyone who will use it. Standards come to us as either decreed by authority or adopted by consensus. Most commercial standards, such as MPEG-2 or Internet Protocol (IP), typically are defined by consensus or authority and self imposed to meet internal or market needs. Organizations that develop commercial standards include:

- Electronic Industries Association (EIA)
- Society of Motion Picture and Television Engineers (SMPTE)
- Institute of Electrical and Electronic Engineers (IEEE)

On the other hand, Governments typically define standards by consensus and impose them by authority. Most of the DoD Agencies and OSD develop standards for use by the Services and Commands.

But why do we need standards? Standards provide a proven, common approach to work and implement a set of best practices (such as the CMMI or Joint Tactics, Techniques and Procedures). They also reduce the learning curve. Can you imagine having to do all the research to create your own set of standards for each project you work on? Nothing would get done and we wouldn't stand a chance at obtaining interoperability.

Standards also facilitate communication among work groups by providing handbooks on how to perform common tasks. For the same reason, they improve the predictability of results, leading to enhanced efficiency and reduced costs. You can also detect potential problems early in the process by using the standards as a gauge for work performance.

Now that we have explained the elements of system engineering, why doesn't everyone use it to solve problems, like architecture?

Why isn't SE popular?

First, SE requires investment. You must invest a portion of your limited budget on the highly visible, up-front costs of the system engineering team.

Secondly, all these rules make the effort seem bureaucratic. Processes, procedures, standards, metrics, and all the other aspects require rigor and discipline to successfully apply.

Thirdly, it seems that all the system engineers generate is paper. Lots of reports, reports, and reports! Trade-off analyses, system engineering management plans, test and evaluation plans, and many more make the policy documentation seem trivial.

Finally and perhaps the biggest complaint about SE is it makes problem areas evident and no one likes to be criticized. If we do our jobs right and do more than criticize, we will provide solutions.

So given all the reasons, you can see why people want to ignore system engineering, but what happens when they do?

What Happens When We Ignore SE?

You can see the symptoms of poor SE:

- confusion over customer mission
- confusion over customer requirements
- failure to document decisions
- point design without options
- conflict between systems and design engineering
- no formal, enforced change control
- floating baseline
- behind schedule
- over budget
- failure to achieve technical requirement
- failure to achieve customer expectation

The result is frayed nerves, late nights, a feeling of not making any progress, let alone accomplishing the tasks and being able to move on to more interesting projects or phases of the current project. I've seen all these symptoms and have experienced the resulting feelings.

Often the problem comes because an insufficient amount of time or funding was allotted to the SE portion of the project. Figure 4-3 shows what happened to a lot of the National Aviation and Space Administration (NASA) programs.[4]

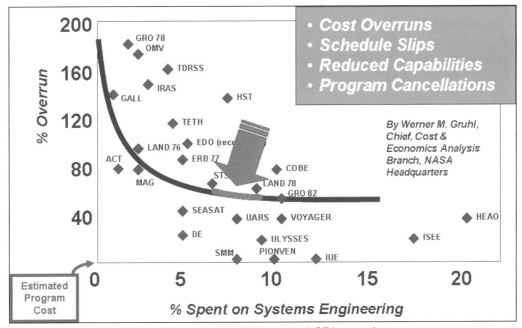

Figure 4-3. Not doing enough SE has a price.

---

[4] Obtained information from James Long, Vitech Corporation in personal communication. Also available in "Managing Requirements," Ivy F. Hooks, located at http://www.complianceautomation.com/papers/ManagingRequirements.pdf

This figure shows that spending from 7-10% on system engineering was necessary and sufficient to keep the program on track. It also shows that it took a lot more than initially budgeted to execute the program (*50% more*). I think this tells you that the lowest bidders had to estimate the costs very low to win the job, but reality caught up to the Government through the engineering change proposal (ECP) process.[5]

What are the key characteristics of a system engineer?

So, recognizing that we need system engineering, what are the characteristics of successful system engineers? First, they must have a strong foundation, including the mastery of systems engineering techniques we discussed above. You can get much of that foundational knowledge from courses and degree programs in system engineering. But to be successful, you need a few enhancements. These enhancements include having:

- real world experience with an operational and systems perspective;
- a grounding in related disciplines (testing, logistics, etc.);
- adequate domain experience (e.g. C4ISR);
- the capability to listen to what's really being said;
- the ability to translate different technical languages; and
- a sense of balance and fairness.

Unfortunately, many people are given the title of system engineer, but don't have these characteristics. The designation SE also has been confused by the advent of a Microsoft Certified System Engineer (MCSE) program that focuses on what I like to call "box-level system engineering." Box-level system engineers have many of the characteristics above, but lack the broader vision of the problem space. That's usually due to the lack of experience or an experience focused solely on developing software or hardware products.

The characteristics for the *architecture-level* system engineer include the ability to see the big picture and ensure that all the pieces conform to that vision. The architecture-level system engineers make successful DoDAF architects.

Ok, I'm sure by now you're wondering if this is a book on system engineering or architectures. *By the way, the answer to that question is yes.*

How does SE apply to Architecture?

System engineering relates to architecture development since architecture provides the broader context for a specific set of systems. In

---

[5] Dan Goldin tried to fix the underbidding problem early in his tenure as Administrator. On one procurement he told all the bidder's to go back and provide realistic costs.

an architecture study, we usually just go down to the level of decomposition where we can specify, at a high-level, the requirements for all the affected systems. In classical system engineering, we start with those high-level requirements and drive the decomposition deeper until we can completely specify the systems. If you can remember that *one person's system is another person's component, is another person's architecture,* you will recognize that the same techniques, processes, tools, and people can do architectures that can do system engineering.

That leads us to our fourth myth.

Myth #4: The Framework was developed to provide architectures as something different from the systems we engineer.

♦ *In reality, the participants in the Framework Panel were all (or mostly) systems engineers. The products are all systems engineering products.*

♦ *The difference between systems and architecture engineering is usually in terms of breadth and depth. Architecture definitions are usually broader and shallower than systems, but the same techniques work for both.*

So, now that we understand the relationship between system engineering and architectures, how do we use system engineering to create our architecture?

How Do We Describe Architectures Using Systems Engineering?

I said earlier in the chapter that we need techniques, processes, and tools to define our methodology for architecture development. Figure 4-4 shows an example from a technique called Model-based System Engineering (MBSE). Note that this diagram captures the sequencing, inputs, and outputs in a single chart.

In addition to having graphical representations of essential architecture elements, the technique will define the set of "bins" (schema) to capture the essential elements of information about the architecture.

An example of the process is shown in Figure 4-5. The process I use can be applied at every level of decomposition through out the lifecycle (and I have used it at each of these levels). I actually use a different, but related process, during the integration and test phase. Perhaps the most important thing about the process is to make it realistic, tailored to the technique and tool use, and as simple as possible.

The tools are very important as well. Tools enhance the efficiency of the team, capture the information required by the standards (such as DoDAF), enforce consistency by applying those same standards, and make the generation of products and reports much easier.

Figure 4-6 shows my tool of choice, Vitech's CORE. It provides a base schema that meets 80-90% of my needs on a wide variety of projects and I've extended the schema to meet the special requirements of almost every project I've worked on. The product's flexibility and its ability to model executable processes have reduced the labor; therefore, the cost required to create architectures significantly.

We will discuss the technique, process and tools in-depth in the next chapter. But I want to finish this chapter with a brief discussion on how to balance between these three competing elements of the methodology.

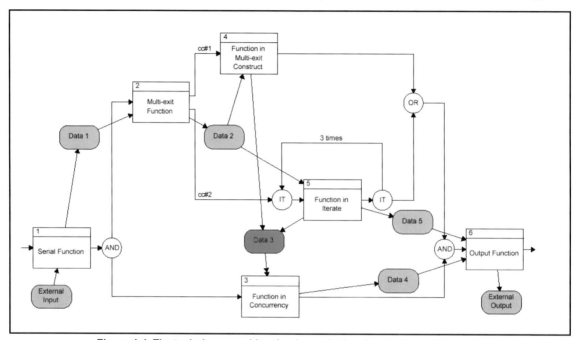

Figure 4-4. The technique provides the theoretical underpinnings of the analysis.

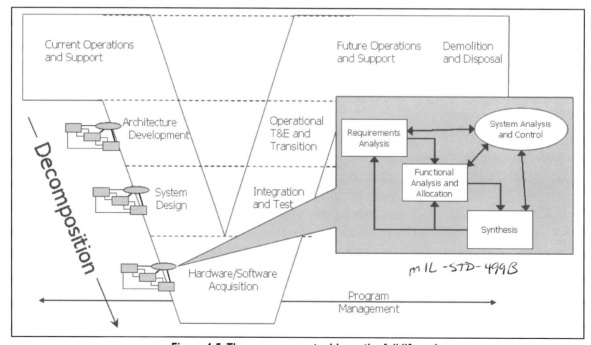

Figure 4-5. The process must address the full lifecycle.

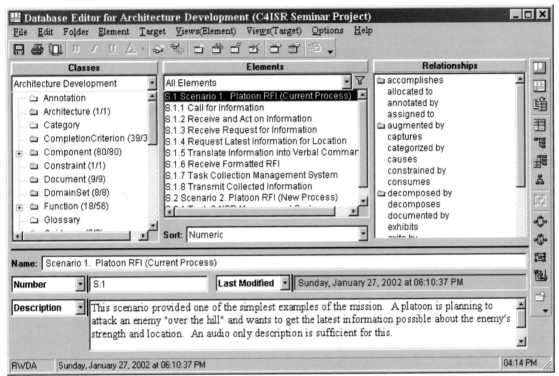

Figure 4-6. The right tools will reduce labor and costs.

Entity - Relationship ?

How Do We Determine the Appropriate Mix of Technique, Process, and Tool(s)?

First, we want to choose the technique(s) you want to use to get the theory right, and then you will want to identify the tools that support the technique. You may find you need more than one to meet all the needs of the theory and the requirements of the DoDAF or other architecture standard you are applying. You then want to select or develop your process. If you select an "off-the-shelf" process, make sure you tailor it to the technique and tools (I'm assuming you would create a new process with the technique and tools in mind automatically … but that could be a bad assumption on my part).

One you've selected these three elements for your methodology, you must optimize all three, balancing between the needs of each to obtain the best solution. Don't be afraid to use a different technique, tool, or process if one doesn't work. Finally, work with your customer to make sure that whatever you produce is what they want. They are not supposed to tell you how to do the job, but they need to have confidence in how you did the work so they can trust the results. *Make sure the customer's in the loop.*

Now let's see the details of my methodology.

5

What Makes a "Good" Methodology?

I said in the previous chapter that there were three elements to the methodology: technique (theory), process, and tools. However, there is a fourth category that we will add to this discussion: people. Once we get through the first three, it should become apparent the kinds of people we need to do this job.

However, before we get to those details, let's review some lessons learned about architectures, or as I like to ask "Why do a lot of our architectures become *shelfware*?"

There are many answers to this question. First, many of the architectures do not fulfill the primary purpose of architectures: to form a bridge between the mission and design. Architectures are often derived from concepts that do not clearly relate to the mission or mission objectives or don't maintain the traceability from those objectives to the design level. They also may not drive the architecture down to a level where designers have clear, verifiable requirements to conduct their design activities.

Another reason for this problem comes from architectures that were done in the abstract, because no end-user was involved in the process. Without end-user involvement, you're almost guaranteed to develop an architecture that doesn't solve the real underlying problems or isn't acceptable to the end-users, because it doesn't communicate in their language. Obviously, you have to be careful not to go to the other extreme, where the end-user drives the entire architecture. In that situation, you may end up with more stovepipes than you started with. Remember the need to balance and optimize.

The next answer I have to this question occurs when you've been tasked to only focus on the "To-Be" without fully understanding the "As-Is." You need to analyze enough of the "As-Is" to understand the root causes of problems or capability gaps. You also need to understand what's already in the process of being changed and what works fine (*if it ain't broke, don't fix it*). By doing enough of the "As-Is" analysis, you won't reinvent working wheels.

Without a good handle on both the "As-Is" and "To-Be", it is very hard to write a good transition plan, and without a transition plan, your architecture doesn't really tell anyone how you're going to get to the Promised Land.

Many architecture development efforts also forget a couple of important system engineering/program management disciplines: configuration management (CM) and quality management (QM). When you have a team of more than one, you have configuration management issues. They apply to the portions of the architecture, just like they do to writing a proposal, developing software, or building an airplane. These are just different scales of the CM problem. The same applies to quality management. You need to ensure consistency of terms and in the use of concepts and processes. Make sure your next architecture project includes these disciplines in the beginning.

One of the problems with the DoDAF is people think they can just create a bunch of diagrams and tables and they're done. That might be true if you ignore one thing: change. I haven't developed an architecture that didn't go through substantial review and changes. If all I had was a "paper" architecture, the change control process alone would be a nightmare. I have seen it occur on a number of architecture projects, even when they use tools. Many of the tools just act as "repositories" for the architecture. What you really need is a database that can generate the products as a result of applying your technique. Then you can use it not only to capture and track changes, but also to answer the myriad of "what if" questions.

My last response to this question is where your architecture lacks complete traceability of all elements, not just requirements. Many people will focus on a "requirements traceability" matrix, which shows how the requirements, such as they are in an architecture project, trace to different functions or systems. But what happens when someone wants to know why a certain change was made and you can't quickly or easily trace it back to a decision that was made two years ago? You may not have been working the architecture at that time. Some other group of people built the ICD, and you're working on the CPD. This happens all the time, particularly with major architectures that seem to have a life of their own. I've found that having a good database tool with a completely linked schema makes all the difference.

So, now that we understand the potential problems with architectures, how do we avoid learning the "lessons learned"[1] again? Well, first, you need to have a clear, simple methodology, with a proven technique, executable process, and powerful set of tools. We will cover these in depth in this chapter.

In addition to methodology, we need to recognize that any project requires planning and continuous re-planning to address changes in the project, and training of the people working on the project. I've seen many projects over the years fail both these items. They think the plan that was developed a year ago should work today. Things change fast,

---

[1] I've heard many people call them "lessons observed." It's clear in most cases no learns a thing.

particularly when you're at war. Your architecture development plan should be reassessed continually as events warrant, but at least every few months. It's better to make minor course corrections than have to make major ones.

The lack of training is appalling, particularly given that any military organization knows how critical training is for operations. Developing an architecture requires training as well. Do not assume that the contractor team rolling in the door knows how to work together as a team. Unless there has been joint training with contractor and Government personnel, they certainly aren't a team with the Government personnel. You need to build an esprit de corps with your entire team and don't forget the new people. They need orientation and process training as well, otherwise a lot of money gets wasted in them coming up to speed.

Perhaps the most important thing to do is to deliver an *executable architecture*. We defined an executable architecture as one that works in Chapter 1. It's real easy to develop one that won't execute. You can draw a bunch of OV-5/OV-6 and SV-4/SV-10 diagrams that will have queuing problems (bottlenecks), activities that need to be performed before other waiting for information (time machine needed!), and insufficient resources (waiting for stuff). Modeling and simulation can resolve these potential problems, before they impact the cost, schedule and/or performance, but an executable architecture requires the use of more rigorous techniques to ensure that you can fully represent the behavior of the architecture.

Now that we understand the problems to avoid, let's discuss the techniques we can use to build an executable architecture.

5.1. What Techniques Should We Use to Build Architectures and Designs?

Over the years, a number of techniques have been developed to model system and software design. These techniques range from the ad hoc viewgraph engineering (a.k.a. death by PowerPoint), a variety of structured analysis techniques (with and without real-time extensions), object-oriented techniques (such as UML), and one you may not be familiar with, Model Based System Engineering (MBSE).

I'll discuss each of the techniques in the following sections, giving pros and cons for each. And I'll tell you which one I like best (and yes, we will spend most of the pages on that one). However, no matter what technique you choose, *make sure it provides a broad, complete foundation for analysis and specification.*

5.1.1 What Is Structured Analysis?

Structured analysis provides a formalism for solving problems using a four step approach: 1) develop a model of the current physical systems; 2) develop a logical model from the physical systems, abstracting out the functional and data elements; 3) change the logical model to meet your new needs; and 4) construct a new physical model from the new logical model.

A variety of structured analysis techniques have been developed over time, including IDEF, Yordon-DeMarco, and Ward & Mellor. Most of these techniques use multiple, linked diagrams to capture and present the essential information about a system or architecture. Structured analysis was adopted early on by the system engineering community. The software engineering community also began to use these methods in the late 1970s, early 1980s and many were adapted to that world, since the "big problem" was software.

Let's take a quick look at a couple of these techniques. The first thing we want to look at is the IDEF or Integration Definition models. Figure 5-1 shows two of the IDEF diagrams[2]: the IDEF 0 that models functional data flow and the IDEF 1X that models data. We saw the IDEF 0 used in Chapter 2 as an example of the OV-5.

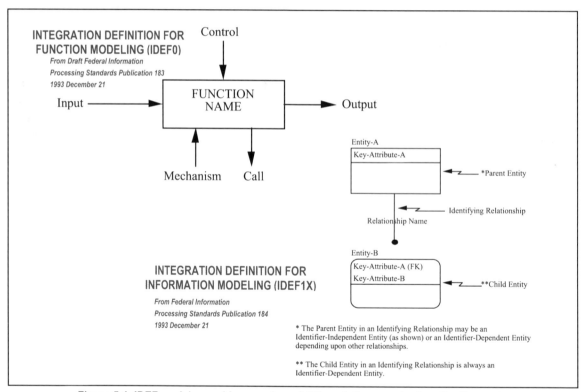

Figure 5-1. IDEF models provide a number of different diagrams to describe the system.

The IDEF 0 captures the data flow (inputs and outputs) between the functions, as well as the "control" flow that isn't transformed, but influences the behavior of the function, and the mechanism that describes how the function is implemented. Note that the sequencing of the functions is not captured on this diagram.

---

[2] "Relationships between Common Graphical Representations in Systems Engineering" (July 2002). Available at http://www.vitechcorp.com/tech_papers.html.

The IDEF 1X looks a lot like the entity-relationship-attribute (ERA) diagram used as the template for the OV-7. That's because it is very similar. It contains additional features, but they start getting too esoteric for this discussion.[3]

The IDEF technique has many more diagrams; so if you want to use this technique, try to become familiar with all of them.

Another structured analysis technique that achieved popularity in the 1980s was the Yourdon[4] data flow diagrams (DFD) and state transition diagrams (STD) (also known as DeMarco diagrams). An example of the DFD is shown in Figure 5-2. This diagram represents the functions as circles (instead of rectangles). The data flows are shown by the lines with arrowheads. The squares represent "external systems" that generate the initial data flows and receive output data for the functions modeled. Perhaps one of the telltale features of this drawing is the lines with words sandwiched in between. These are called *data stores* or *data repositories* and capture where data can be stored and retrieved. Hence, they can represent a database.

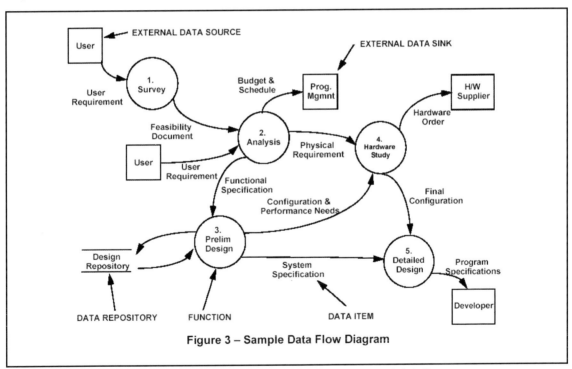

Figure 3 – Sample Data Flow Diagram

Figure 5-2. DFD provide another way to represent data flow.

We saw this same kind of diagram as the template for the SV-4, which is where the Framework panel originally got the idea (I was told these were just a bunch of system engineering diagrams).

---

[3] For more details on the IDEF modeling I recommend Dennis Buede's book, "The Engineering Design of Systems," published by John Wiley & Sons, Inc., 2000.

[4] See Edward Yourdon's classic textbook, "Modern Structured Analysis," published by Prentice-Hall, Inc. 1989.

We also saw the STDs in the OV-6b and SV-10b DoDAF products. To round out the group, Yourdon also used the ERA diagram, which is the basis for the OV-7. So you can now clearly see from where the DoDAF diagrams come. Of course that's only half the DoDAF story. Now let's talk Object-Oriented (O-O).

5.1.2 What Are Object-Oriented Techniques?[5]

In the 1990s, in the middle of the Internet boom, several software designers decided to create a new approach to the problem called object-oriented design and analysis. They used diagrams similar to the IDEF and Yourdon diagrams, including the state transition diagrams (STD), but the primary diagram was the *class* diagram. An example of a class diagrams is shown in Figure 5-3.

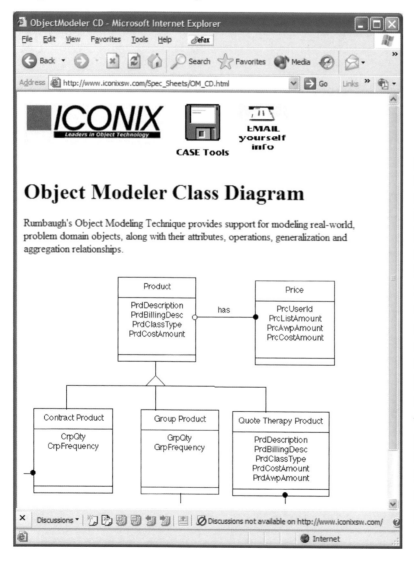

Figure 5-3. Class diagrams hold the key to object analysis .

The class diagram defines the attributes and methods (functions) that an object will have. Classes are an abstract grouping, where as the objects are the *instantiation* of the class. The diagram also contains relationships, like an ERA diagram, but the notation provides inheritance properties, as well. Children classes inherit the attributes and methods of the parent class.

---

[5] Much of the information for this section was derived from "Understanding UML – The Developer's Guide with a Web-Based Application in Java," by Paul Harmon and Mark WatsonMorgan Kaufmann Publishers, Inc., 1998 and various websites.

During the 1990s, three competing notations were developed (Booch, Rumbaugh, and Jacobson). A consortium of Rational Software, Microsoft, and the Object Management Group (OMG) standardized the notation and set of diagrams into what's now called the Unified Modeling Language (UML). Figure 5-4 shows icons for many of the diagrams included in UML. This technique uses many of the previously discussed techniques, including the state, activity, and class diagrams. It also adds in the use case diagram we saw in the OV-5 discussion in Chapter 2. UML has become very popular in the software engineering community. You can't go to Border's or Barnes and Noble without finding row after row of UML books.

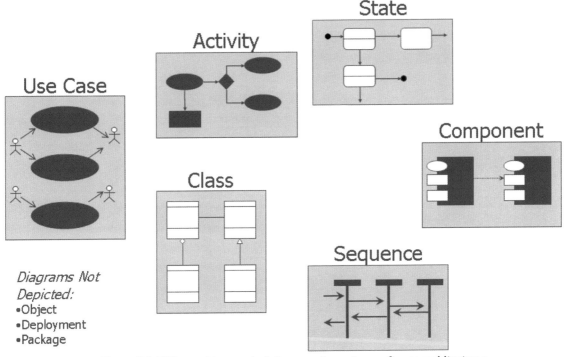

Figure 5-4. UML provides a set of diagrams to capture software architectures.

As this technique gained in popularity, many system engineers attempted to apply this technique to systems, and now architectures, with some limited success. It has caused a running argument between the traditional structured analysis community and the UML practitioners. The argument focuses around the fact that in UML (like all O-O techniques) you must define the objects first. This can cause you to be tied too tightly to today's objects, when you want to build tomorrow's systems. For software, which has a much shorter lifecycle, this isn't a big problem, but for systems and architectures where we measure the lifecycle in decades, it can be quite troublesome. Hence, the structured analysts believe that addressing the functions first, and then using them to define the objects, is a better way to go. I must admit that I'm in the structured analysis camp, but another effort holds out hope of bringing the two camps together. It's called SysML.

System Modeling Language (SysML) is an offshoot of UML notation with adjustments and additional diagrams. The activity diagram is being adjusted to add activity (functional) sequencing, thus enabling diagram execution (which is already available in MBSE, as we will show in the next section.) They also want to add diagrams to capture requirements and parametrics (e.g., performance parameters) and relate them to the other architectural elements. You can follow this activity on the website *www.sysml.org*. Figure 5-5 shows an example of these changes.[6]

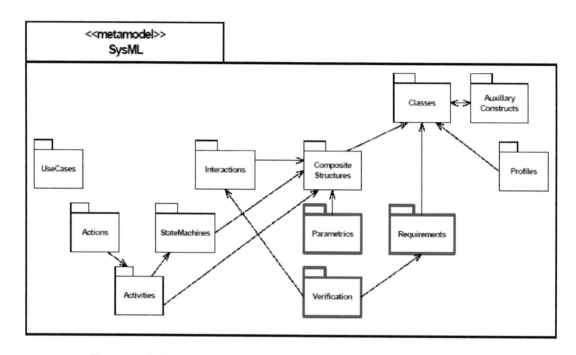

Figure 5-5. SySML adds parametrics, requirements and verification classes to UML

As you can see, these techniques all have some holes in them for the use in architectures and system engineering. Some are new (UML) and some are not even implemented yet (SysML). I find all these techniques intriguing and try to follow their development, but the biggest problem I've had with the techniques is they all seem to be oriented toward a diagram world that's limited to 8½ x 11 sheets of paper.

The technique I've used for the past 15 years has yet to be shown lacking, at least in theory, to meet any architectural, system engineering, or software development problems I've encountered over that time. I've even used it on test and evaluation projects. So what's this technique? Today it's called Model-Based System Engineering.[7]

---

[6] These figures and information on SysML were obtained from a briefing provided at www.sysml.org entitled "Systems Modeling Language" dated November 19, 2003.

[7] The term MBSE was coined by Vitech Corporation and comes from a long history of techniques, beginning with Software Requirements Engineering Methodology (SREM) in the late 1960s and early 1970s. The authors of this language include Mr. James Long and Ms. Margaret Dyer. More on this history will be presented in the next section.

5.1.3 What Is Model-Based System Engineering (MBSE)?

As its name indicated, MBSE uses a modeling approach to system engineering, as opposed to a diagram-based approach, as most of these other techniques. The basis for the technique comes from the recognition that the job of the system engineer (and architect) is to translate abstract concepts and statements of need into a more concrete, structured language that a system hardware or software designer can derive the requirements needed to develop solutions to the problems at hand.

Figure 5-6 shows the structured language meta-model,[8] based on ERA and its equivalent to the English language. MBSE defines a set of elements (aka entities), relationships, and attributes, but also adds *attributes on relationships* to provide the equivalent of adverbs and recognizes that not all concepts are communicated in words, but also in diagrams. If it wasn't implemented correctly, just using ERA wouldn't be anything spectacular. The authors[9] of MBSE have created a complete set of elements that capture the essence of almost any system. They recently in 2005 updated that schema to include the latest DoDAF elements.

Language Elements	English Equivalent	Example
Element	Noun	• OriginatingRequirement • Function • Component • ...
Relationship	Verb	• OriginatingRequirement traces to Functions • Functions are allocated to Components • ...
Attribute	Adjective	• Creator • Creation Date • Text Description • ...
Attribute of Relationship	Adverb	• amount of Resource consumed by Function • acquire available (hold partial) Resource for Function • ...
Structure Enables Executability	Graphics/ Drawings	• Graphic Views: Behavior, FFBD, N2, ER, ERA, Hierarchies, IDEF0, Physical Block

Figure 5-6. MBSE provides a robust language for architecture definition.

---

[8] This figure and the other presented in this section were provided by Vitech as part of a joint tutorial entitled "Developing Executable Architectures for Systems of Systems (SoS) using DoDAF," by Dr. Steven H. Dam and Mr. David A. Long, at the SETE Conference 2005, in Brisbane, Australia. Vitech has granted permission to reproduce this and the other Vitech copyrighted materials contained in this book.

[9] The current authors of MBSE are Mr. James Long, Mr. David Long and Ms. Margaret Dyer of Vitech Corporation. Note that two of these three were original authors of SREM.

So part of the modeling in MBSE is language, but the structures that enable executability are models of control, interfaces, and components. Figure 5-7 shows these models . The combination of these three models, which use the language discussed above, provides the necessary and sufficient models to completely specify a system.

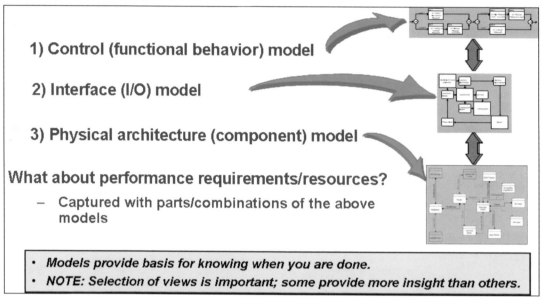

1) **Control (functional behavior) model**

2) **Interface (I/O) model**

3) **Physical architecture (component) model**

What about performance requirements/resources?

   – Captured with parts/combinations of the above models

- *Models provide basis for knowing when you are done.*
- *NOTE: Selection of views is important; some provide more insight than others.*

Figure 5-7. MBSE provides the models needed for specifying architectures.

Notice that the first model captures control or functional sequencing. Most techniques provide only a limited way to represent the logical sequencing of functions, and hence, architect/engineers only use that limited set (primarily serial processing, with some feedback loops). The end result is a poor representation of the robust logic of a real system.

MBSE avoids this problem by defining a complete set of logical constructs, as shown in Figure 5-8. These constructs include the standard serial (sequence) and parallel (concurrency) , which are constructs you can find in IDEF models, but it also includes loops (with loop exits so you can know when to end a loop), iterates (over a defined domain set), ORs (select and multiple exit), and the replicate. The replicate construct provides a way to deal with an arbitrary number of identical functions (which can represent systems) in parallel, under a common control element. An example of this would be the functions performance by airplanes in an air traffic controllers (ATC) sector (Function A in the diagram) and the ATC personnel (Function B).

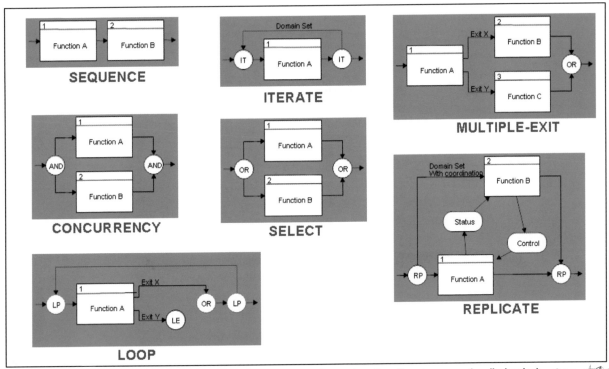

Figure 5-8. The complete set of constructs necessary to capture functional sequencing (behavior). *control*

This powerful set of logical constructs provides the means for capturing the behavior of your architecture, system, or software. Many software developers try to avoid modeling the control logic. Their world is focused on inputs and outputs.[10] Since their primary goal is to control their environment, architects and system engineers must model functional behavior. In the software world, the big complaint is about "undocumented features," which you might call "bugs", but these "bugs" come from programming them in and are usually unintentional. In most commercial computer systems, when you encounter a software bug, you can reboot and no real damage is done. However, for the kinds of systems we build at DoD, bugs can be fatal … literally.

Now, let's get back to MBSE. MBSE also provides a means to combine the interface diagram inputs and outputs, including a special case of input called a trigger, with the control model to create a behavior diagram. Figure 5-9 shows an example of the behavior diagram[11] that applies a number of these logical constructs.

The behavior diagram or enhanced function flow block diagram (EFFBD) enables you to see how the inputs and output affect the functional sequencing and vice versa. Figure 5-9 is read from left to

---

[10] Most code in my experience is all about inputs and outputs (I/O), since they make us 80-90% of the code. If you don't believe me take a good look at the modern programming languages like Java. Their class libraries are mostly about I/O.

[11] From "Relationships between Common Graphical Representations in Systems Engineering" (July 2002). Available at http://www.vitechcorp.com/tech_papers.html.

117

right.[12] The control lines enable the function, but it can not execute until it receives a trigger (unless it has no triggers as input). The execution then proceeds for the time allotted; the function or the time takes it for the decomposition of the function to complete. In the parallel branch shown (the AND construct), both branches execute in parallel, but must end together before proceeding beyond the end of the AND (to execute function 6, the Output Function in the diagram). Function 2, the Multi-exit Function, enables the execution to go down one path or (exclusively) the other. The branching between the top or bottom path can be determined probabilistically, decomposition, or script. If the bottom of the two OR branches executes Function 5, the "Function in Iterate" will execute three times (since that's the domain set shown). Notice how both the top OR branch and the bottom one produce the green Data 3 item. The green indicates that this item is a *trigger* element. So, Function 3 can not execute until it receives that trigger, which it will receive from either path. You can imagine how easy it would be to forget to draw the output of that trigger from one or the other functions above. If you forgot that one little line, the diagram would no longer execute. Can you imagine how easy that would be to do on a large number of such diagrams? So the capability to execute the diagram will be very important to the ability to verify that the logic works.

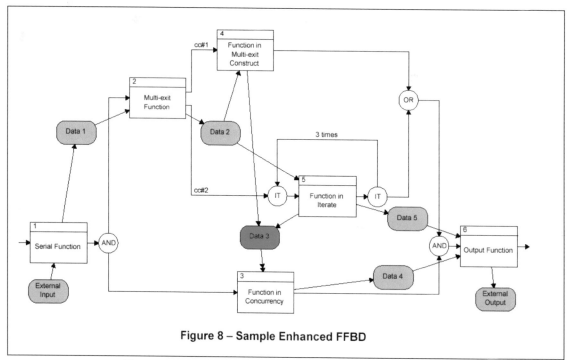

Figure 8 – Sample Enhanced FFBD

Figure 5-9. MBSE captures control and data flow in a single diagram.

---

[12] The original behavior diagrams were drawn from top to bottom. This approach was implemented in a tool called RDD-100.

OK, so now that I've explained this behavior diagram, you must be thinking, "what's this got to do with DoDAF?"

Well, it just so happens that this behavior diagram contains all the information needed to create a number of the DoDAF products. Figure 5-10 shows the many faces of behavior. From the EFFBD, you can create the OV-5b/SV-4b, which show the data flows between operational activities or system functions. As you may recall (if not go back and look at Chapter 4), the hierarchy diagrams are also part of the OV-5/SV-4, and they can also be seen resulting for the behavior modeling.

If you want the pure timing and sequencing diagrams (OV-6c/SV-10c), that's the same as the classical function flow block diagram (FFBD). You can also derive a text view, where the attributes of the operational activity or system function can be captured. Resources can also be associated with the functions through a Resource element, its relationships to functions (*captured by* or *consumed by*), and the attributes on those relationships (*amount*).

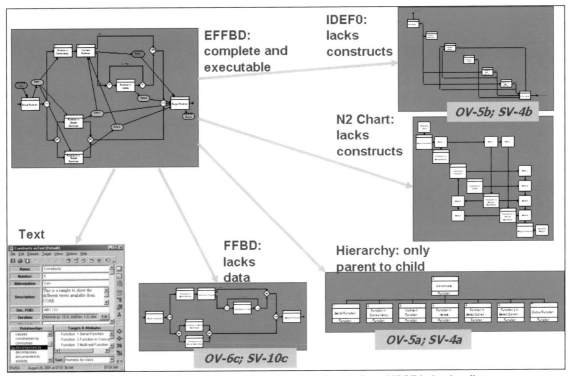

Figure 5-10. DoDAF products can be extracted directly from MBSE behavior diagrams.

So with behavior diagrams, we get the first two of the MBSE models, but what about the component model? MBSE let's you start from the top with an architecture and drill down to systems, subsystems, components, sub-components, etc. until you can complete specify the physical elements of the architecture. Figure 5-11 shows an example of this physical decomposition in a simple hierarchy diagram. It begins as high as you want to start (the Universe may be too high, but it let's you know that you can establish the context of your architecture at any level). From this diagram, you can determine the systems of interest, hence, scoping the problem or establishing the *context* for the problem. You can also use another diagram to show how the physical components of your architecture communicate (via links – interfaces or needlines depending whether your modeling operational elements/nodes or system elements/nodes). An example of this physical block diagram is shown in Figure 5-12. The links constrain the flow of data elements (they call them *Items* to keep it general, since it can model physical object interchanges, not just data).

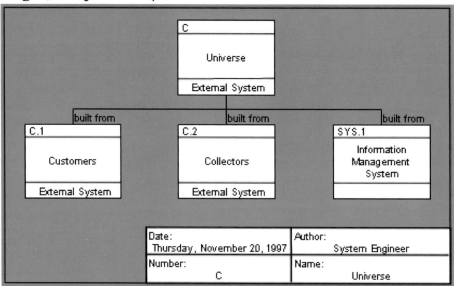

Figure 5-11. The MBSE component model is captured as a hierarchy diagram ...

When functions (from the behavior diagram) are allocated to these components, and the items (also from the behavior diagram) are allocated to the links, the timing and sequencing is affected, thus adding the *physical constraints* to the modeling.

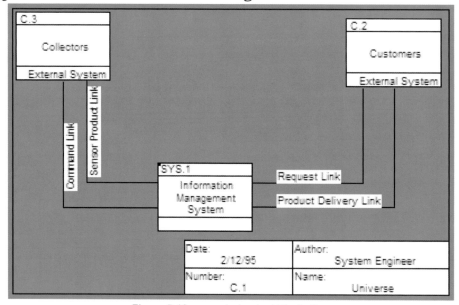

Figure 5-12. ... and physical block diagram.

The end result of applying these models provides a complete traceability, of all elements within the MBSE schema. Figure 5-13 shows a traceability hierarchy, color coded so you can see each of the element classes immediately. The green are physical components, the purple are functions, and the white are requirements. Other factors needed for the decision process have also been included in this diagram, including issues (and decisions), risks (with mitigation), performance metrics, and constraints. With this traceability you can answer the "what if questions," such as "what if I need to replace a component (e.g. the green box with the red circle)?" or "what if I change a requirement (e.g. the white box in the red circle)?" The first order answers to those questions can immediately be obtained from this diagram, by looking up or down the hierarchy to determine what elements are affected by the change. Now you don't just have an architectural modeling technique, you have a decision aid!

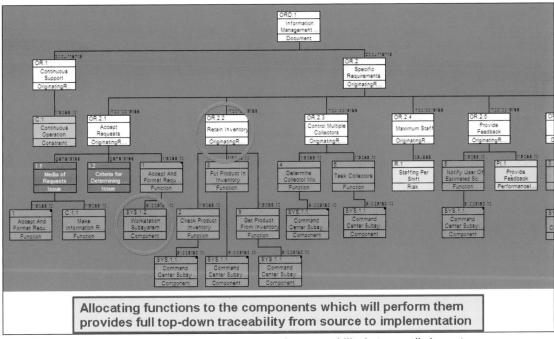

Figure 5-13. MBSE provides complete traceability between all elements.

Now that we understand the different techniques, let's focus in on one of the most important topics of this book: executable architectures.

5.1.4. How Do We Develop Executable Architectures and Designs?

The need for executable models becomes clear when we realize that we can draw diagrams that look OK, but in reality, don't work. Most of the techniques discussed above use static diagrams to represent process flows. Static diagrams may or may not actually work, since in reality many of the processes interact with one another and functional decomposition can miss critical interfaces. Simulation enables the execution of these models, thus ensuring that the design is executable. Therefore, having a technique that provides the necessary contracts for timing and sequencing and the semantic meaning for execution becomes imperative. The DoDAF recognizes this fact and has defined the term executable architectures in Volume I, Section 7.3.

Recent work to expand the topic of executable architectures for DoDAF 2.0 has been lead by the Defense Modeling and Simulation Organization (DMSO). Figure 5-14 show the levels of executability under consideration for this next version of the DoDAF.[13]

The first two levels are captured in the current DoDAF as the OV-5/SV-4 (structure) and OV-6/SV-10 (time ordered). Classical modeling and simulation (M&S) falls into the next two categories, time scheduled and time functional. In fact, many of the large scale simulators, such as the ones for flight or tanks, fit primarily into the time functional level. Those simulations cost millions to develop and have terrific benefits for training.

For architecture development, no one wants to spend millions on verification of the architectural design. In fact, it would be difficult to create the large-scale simulation in this case, since we probably don't know enough to provide the fidelity of information needed. Hence, we need to have models that we can verify at a reasonable cost and quickly using discrete event simulation.

Levels DMSO

Level Description	Analysis Facilitated	Mathematical Representation	Character
Structure	Allows Assessment of gaps and overlaps	Relational Models (lists), database technology	Static Analysis
Time Ordered	Allows assessment of behavior without resource contention (queuing)	Directed Graphs (e.g. Petri Net)	Static Deterministic Time Behavior
Time Scheduled	Operational efficiencies and system performance trade-offs	Queuing Network (e.g. temporal Petri Net, Discrete Event Simulation)	Dynamic, non-deterministic time behavior
Time Functional	Allows representation of the "architectural elements" in the context of "platforms" best represented by continuous simulation	Traditional M&S Integrated with continuous models HWIL, HIL, Real time	Dynamic Instantiated architecture

Figure 5-14. Different levels of executablity.

---

[13] From "Executables Overlay" presentation by Mr. Ken Atkinson, DMSO, dated 28 April 2005, presented at the IDGA DoD Architectures conference, Silver Springs, MD.

What are the characteristics of a technique that can be modeled as a discrete event simulation? Well, let's look at the "dimensions" of an architecture's behavior. Figure 5-15 shows an abstract cloud, which represents an architecture. The behavior dimensions are primarily data flow, functional sequencing, and time. The OV-5/SV-4 characterize the data flow, which for simple systems with sequential flow may be sufficient. However, for more complex systems, which all architectures are, it can be very misleading, but neither of these diagrams captures the time dimension well and certainly don't handle the other dimensions (resources, data size, and interface constraints).

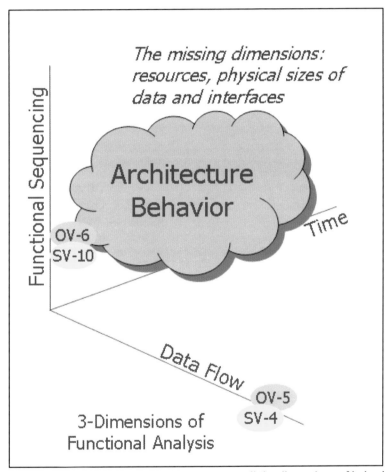

Figure 5-15. DoDAF products do not capture all the dimensions of behavior.

The key to obtaining the time dimension is to apply a technique that will enable the creation of executable models. MBSE has this capability. By executing the behavior model, we can see the actions of the activities/functions over time, including the effects on resources. Figure 5-16 shows a resulting timeline,[14] with resource usage from executing a MBSE behavior diagram. The yellow lines indicate functions enabled,

---

[14] From "Relationships between Common Graphical Representations in Systems Engineering" by Jim Long, Vitech Corporation, (July 2002). Available at http://www.vitechcorp.com/infocenter/papers.

but waiting for a trigger for execution. The green (and teal) show function execution times. The red in the resources show where there weren't enough resources to perform the functions. The corresponding red violet sections of the function timelines show the corresponding time delays as the functions waited for resources.

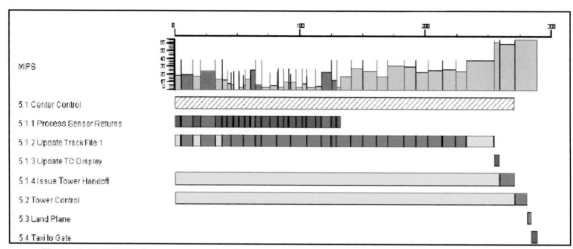

Figure 5-16. MBSE discrete event simulation provides a more realistic timing and sequencing analysis.

You may think: "Well I may need this for a complicated process, but most of my processes are simple. I'll just model them with OV-5 and not worry about the timing and sequencing." If you do that, you may find out (often too late) it was a mistake.

Let's take a simple example. A basic service-oriented architecture (SOA – the buzzword of 2005) can be drawn as in Figure 5-17.

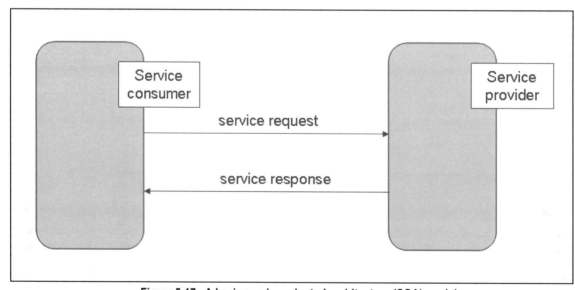

Figure 5-17. A basic service oriented architecture (SOA) model.

This most basic form of SOA has a *service consumer* requesting a service and a *service provider* responding to the request (hopefully with the service, at least eventually). Let's model this using the IDEF 0 (a basic OV-5 product). The result might look like Figure 5-18. Do we think this is executable the way it is shown? Since we really don't know what the timing and sequencing of the functions would be, the answer is a definite maybe, although one might think this to be a serial process.

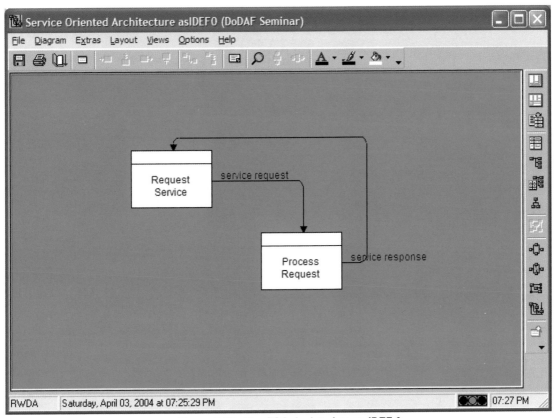

Figure 5-18. The SOA depicted as an IDEF 0.

However, in general, the service consumer and service provider operate independently of one another, one requesting lots of other services and the other (hopefully) providing their service to other customers (otherwise they probably wouldn't be in business long.)

That means that the data flows shown in Figure 5-18 must be triggers (i.e. the functions need the triggering events from each other to complete their activities.) So, let's see how this scenario would look as an EFFBD.

Figure 5-19 shows the more general case as an EFFBD using the MBSE methodology. We said that MBSE behavior diagrams can be tested through simulation, so if we use the tool's built-in discrete event simulation capability (call CORESim) and hit the run button, we get the result shown in Figure 5-20. It looks like there was a problem. If we expand the error box (Figure 5-21), it shows the error message. The message (in plain English) says that both functions were waiting for their respective triggers. What this means is we were missing a function! We need to have transmit and receive functions (probably for both, but for simplicity we will only show the one). The fixed EFFBD (Figure 5-22) is then executed again, with the result showing that it works (Figure 5-23).

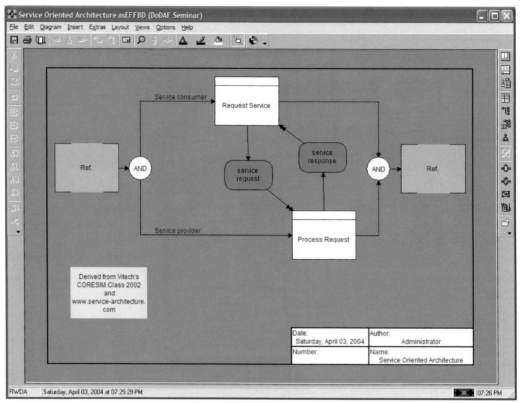

Figure 5-19. SOA example as an EFFBD.

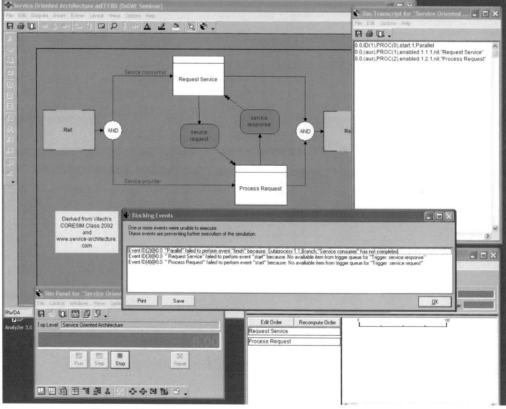

Figure 5-20. The result of executing the diagram – a problem is found.

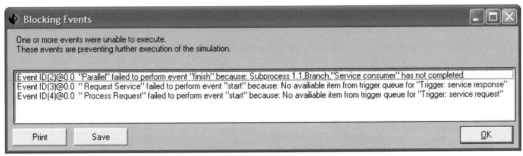

Figure 5-21. Both functions waiting on triggers.

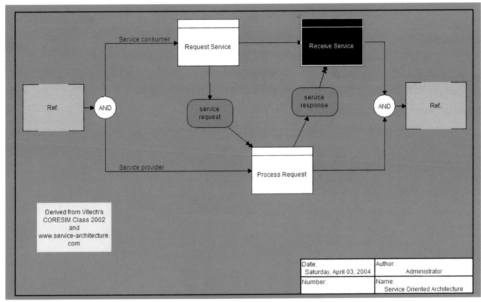

Figure 5-22. Problem fixed?

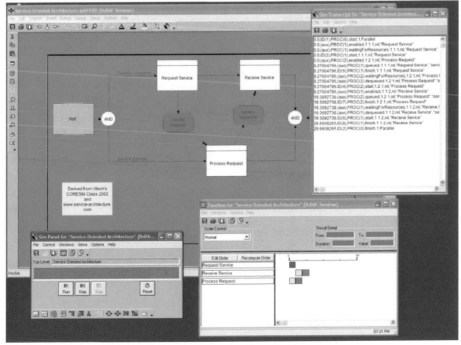

Figure 5-23. Problem fixed – yes.

Now I'm sure that you may have been able to see this problem, but could you find such an error in a more complex case, such as the one diagramed in Figure 5-24? What about one with three levels of decomposition? What about the effect of resources or low bandwidth communications? Clearly, this kind of modeling *and simulation* is essential for rapidly developing architecture models and verifying that they work.

However, most architecture projects never get this far. They begin and end with DoDAF products and never fully model the real architecture, leaving all the problems for the next level of analysis. If you're lucky, they will catch problems in system design. Unless someone goes back and does the complete architectural analysis, it's unlikely that they will catch architectural problems, like interoperability and meeting all the mission objectives. The next time such an error would be caught is operational test and evaluation (OT&E), when – if we're lucky – we only have to settle for reduced capabilities.

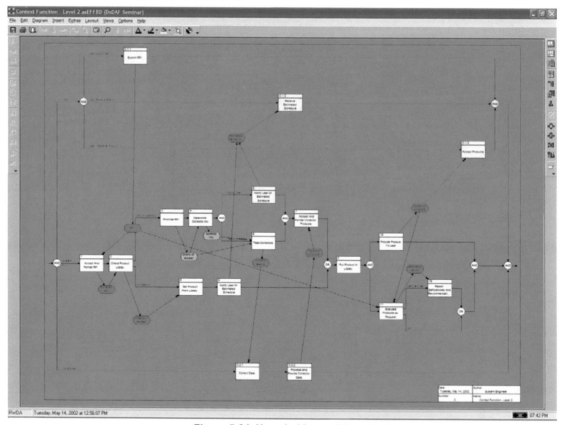

Figure 5-24. How do I know this works?

To ensure that we do a better job of architectural modeling, we need to think about the criteria for choosing a technique. The last sub-section of this discussion of techniques addresses the question: How do we select a good technique?

5.1.5 How Do We Select a Technique?

To select our technique we need to come up with a reasonable set of characteristics that we can use as evaluation criteria. My list is as follows:

- Addresses your full lifecycle
- Integrates a set of processes
- Provide executable results
- Uses appropriate software tools
- Communicates well to all audiences
- Extends ability to adjust to specific needs
- Has been applied successfully

Since the architecture starts the development lifecycle and OT&E, which evaluates the resulting systems by the criteria developed by the architecture, ends the developmental part of the lifecycle, I've found having a technique (MBSE) that applies across the entire lifecycle is essential. I've even used this technique to support operations and maintenance, as well as disposal (of nuclear waste.) It works everywhere I've tried it.

It needs to tie together the project management processes, including risk management (RM), configuration management (CM), and other processes. I've used it to capture processes and create procedure documentation.

Since we just spent an entire section on executability, I hope that one's obvious.

"Uses appropriate software tools" is all about not having to do this manually. Diagram execution requires someway to create the discrete event simulation from the diagram, but it's much more than that. You need to have a schema and database to capture the information and maintain all the relationships. Without a tool that implements the technique, it would be very difficult to maintain the design.

"Communicates well to all audiences" is a tough one. I'm not sure that any of these techniques meet this criteria. *All* is too broad. Just like the OV-1 may be the only DoDAF product that communicates well to just about everyone, but only because they are used to the viewgraph wars. The technique itself may not meet this criteria, but it should enable you to capture the information so that you can satisfy all audiences with the information they need. I've found that tables communicate well, so you can use the information gathered by your technique to fill in the tables. That would then meet this criteria.

"Extends ability to adjust to specific needs" means that you can extend the schema or adjust it in ways, such as adding attributes or changing the name of an element. The MBSE technique I use provides the 80-90% solution, but has the ability to be extended so that I can fill in the gaps.

The last of my criteria "Has been successfully applied" is key. I've seen over the past 25 years a number of techniques come and go, but they tend to get over sold, and then people are disillusioned and go looking for the next "silver bullet." Until I see proof that the new technique is better, I'd rather stick with something I know works. I don't think UML meets these criteria, and we don't know what SysML will do for us until it becomes real. In the mean time, I'll stick with something that's been working since 1969 (MBSE).

But my opinions, however fact based, are mine. Whatever your criteria, do with it what good system engineers have always done – run a trade study. My trade study for techniques is shown in Figure 5-25.

Do your own.

Criteria	IDEF	MBSE	UML
Addresses your full life cycle	Yes (if all 15 views are developed)	Yes	No (mostly software focused)
Integrates a set of processes (e.g., SE, Risk, CM, ...)	Not directly (i.e., no Risk view)	Yes	No
Provide executable results	No	Yes	No
Uses appropriate software tools	Yes	Yes	Yes
Communicates well to all audiences	Focused on a technical audience	Provides insight into processes	Well understood by software developers
Extends ability to adjust to specific needs	No	Yes	Yes
Has been applied successfully	Yes	Yes	No?

Figure 5-25. Use *your* criteria to select a technique.

Now that we have a good idea about the techniques available for architecture development, let's see what tools are available for doing the job.

5.2. What Tools Support DoDAF and SE Design and Development?

We said that the next step in developing a methodology was the selection of a tool that implements the technique. Perhaps you didn't realize you need a tool to execute the DoDAF, and in a sense, you're right, but only if you have a tremendous amount of resources to keep track of all the data elements. That leads us to our 5th myth. Although the Framework doesn't require a specific tool, it becomes fairly obvious, when looking at the requirements of the Framework, for the need to

> **Myth #5: Using the Framework doesn't require the use of a database tool**
> ◆ *In reality, when looking at the "AV-2, Integrated Dictionary" essential product, a database becomes necessary in dealing with all the data. The C4ISR Core Architecture Data Model (CADM) provides a (complex, IDEF-based) schema for this database. However, no tool was directed, since the group believed that sufficient COTS tools would do the job*

capture the information in some kind of repository, preferably a database.

In our DoDAF course, one of the favorite segments is the discussion of various tools, which includes pros and cons of each. Since that information changes rather rapidly, I'll provide a brief discussion of the tools available today (circa Winter 2006), but I highly recommend before you start your next architecture project that you survey the tools out there. I can almost guarantee that they've changed.

5.2.1 What Tools Are Available?

You have a choice from a wide variety of tool types, including drawing tools, database/repository tools, modeling and simulation tools, and visualization tools. No single product has everything you need (let alone want), so we're looking at a toolset, but tool interoperability is a big issue that we will also address in this discussion.

So what do the tools do for us? They help us keep track of the variety of information and enable processes to be executed more efficiently. There's a long list of tools out there, including:

- Proforma (www.proformacorp.com)
- CORE (www.vitechcorp.com)
- Metis (www.troux.com)
- System Architect (http://government.popkin.com/)
- Rational Rose (http://www-306.ibm.com/software/rational/)
- NetViz (www.netviz.com)
- DOORS/TAU (www.telelogic.com)
- SLATE (http://www.sdrc.com/slate/index.shtml)
- ARIS (www.ids-scheer.com/us/)
- Rhapsody (www.ilogix.com)

I've included the websites for these (the most current ones I have). You will find a number of them difficult to locate with Google or some other search engine due to the commonality of the name (e.g. SLATE, DORS, ARIS, ...). All these tools have some capabilities to produce DoDAF products; some even have special facilities, templates, reports, or user interfaces tailored to the DoDAF. Many have built-in modeling and simulation capabilities (e.g., Proforma, CORE, SLATE). Many use UML as a basis (e.g., Rational Rose, TAU, Rhapsody).

Other tools claim to be "methodology independent" or have support for many methodologies. I'm always suspicious of such claims; since to develop a useful tool, you have to at least have an idea of the information you will gather and the output needed. Hence, the tool developer needs to have some technique, and even process, in mind when creating the tool.

The bottom line is that you need to choose the tool that best implements the technique you want to use. Since the mid 1990's, I have used a combination of CORE and NetViz for my architecture work.[15] CORE implements Model-Based System Engineering (MBSE). CORE (by the way it's not an acronym) was designed as a system engineering tool that focuses on functional analysis. The tool provides an integrated design repository that enables traceability between requirements, functional models, and system design elements. CORE's database schema may be modified to customize the tool to support customer needs and facilitate tool integration. The executable diagrams, which we saw in the discussion on techniques, provide a rapid way to verify the logic of the design. CORE has a tailored DoDAF schema (see Figure 5-26) and reports for just about all the DoDAF products. Its powerful scripting language enables you to quickly create your own special reports, tailored to your customer's specific needs. The one place that I find CORE weak is in the "pretty pictures" area. The diagrams it produces are great for system engineers, but they may not communicate well to decision makers (who don't want to see function flow block diagrams) or software developers (who expect to see UML).

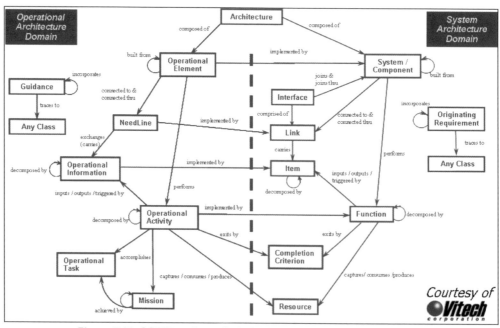

Figure 5-26. CORE's schema includes DoDAF elements and relationships.

---

[15] Prior to the release of CORE 1.0, I used a tool called RDD-100, which implemented the same technique, although at that time it was called SREM.

NetViz (which stands for network visualization) is used by military personnel all over the world to graphically depict operational architectures and logistical scenarios. NetViz has icons for almost every piece of electronics and military gear you can imagine. For ones they don't have, you can easily add them to the catalog and then use them throughout the diagrams. Each icon has attributes that you can define, thus enabling the capture of all kinds of information about a particular piece of hardware or software.

With NetViz you can create the SV-1 and SV-2 diagrams, with its intuitive graphical workspace, drill down capability, and connectivity views. You can use the data embedded in your NetViz projects to create other critical elements of a comprehensive C4I documentation project, like OV-1s (Operational Concept Diagrams) and OV-3s (Information Exchange Matrices). I was able to create a link between CORE and NetViz using a comma separated values file. More sophisticated API to API solutions should be available, although I find CORE's ability to hyperlink to external text and graphics sufficient for my needs.

The one problem with both these tools and all the others is the lack of standardization of information between tools. OSD has been developing the Core Architecture Data Model (CADM) to help this problem, but has run into both difficulties in the complexity of the schema and vendor acceptance of it as a "standard." Using CADM and XML (extensible markup language), OSD has worked hard to convince tool manufacturers to adopt this standard. OSD is using it as a means to develop and deploy a data repository called DARS (the DoD Architecture Repository System), as depicted in Figure 5-27.[16]

However, to date (Winter 2006), only one tool has achieved CADM XML certification, Proforma. So it's not clear how much the tool manufacturers are following their lead. We will see.

As such, we've been investigating the use of another tool, called MD Workbench, Sodius, Inc. (see Figure 5-28) to solve the tool interoperability problem.[17] MD Workbench uses ERA as the "meta-meta-model" and then creates rules to transform one schema to another. The great benefit of this approach comes from its ability to transform not only the data, but the graphics as well. Hence you can convert a UML diagram into a EFFBD and go from there. SODIUS is a value-added reseller (VAR) for Vitech in France, so the rules for CORE and a number of other tools already exist.

---

[16] Presented by Mr. Truman Parmele, OSD/NII at the IDGA DoD Architectures Conference February 24, 2004

[17] See the SODIUS website at http://www.sodius.fr/html/us/mdworkbench.htm.

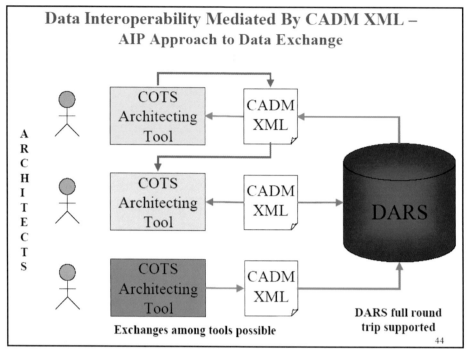

Figure 5-27. OSD's near term plan for tool interoperability – define a "standard:" CADM XML.

Figure 5-28. MD Workbench provides a transformation engine to aid tool interoperability.

We end this subsection with one more myth about tools. Myth #6 continues to be a problem for those of us who don't think one tool can do the job. Many DoD organizations have tried to standardize on a tool and they are discovering that one size doesn't fit all (you'd think that lesson would have been learned long ago).

Myth #6: DoD Has Mandated the Use of a Particular Tool

♦ *Although much discussion of this occurred during the development of the preceding framework (C4ISR Architecture Framework, 2.0), it was decided that DoD would be better served by not "picking a winner"*

♦ *This resulted in a large number of tools being developed for the market*

♦ *OSD/NII has defined the CADM XML standard for interoperability between tools*

5.2.2 How Do We Select the Right Tools?

Just like in the selection of a technique, you need to establish criteria for choosing the tools. The following are my set of criteria and explanation.

The first and foremost is the tools should support your chosen technique. This seems obvious, but people get enamored with tools (particularly customers and managers) that don't really do the complete job; you still need to use your tools. Use something like MD Workbench to put the results into a different tool, if necessary.

Second, the tool should provide several integrated functions, including parsing (document capture), database queries, and report generation. You don't really want to be dependent on too many separate tools to do these things; otherwise the database gets out of synch too easily.

Third, the tool must employ rule-based standards so that you can be sure that you are meeting the requirements of the technique. For example, if your tool creates IDEF 0 diagrams, it should tell you when you've violated the 3 to 6 boxes per diagram rule.

Fourth, having standards also helps to enforce consistency. Consistency of the inputs is usually a combination of procedures and the tool. Most tools enable the creation of input "screens' that limit the kinds of inputs For example, if you must have a hierarchical number, it should check to make sure it meets that criterion.

Fifth, I like to have a single integrated, common database for storing the information. If you have more than one, synchronization and configuration management become big issues. I used one tool a long time ago that had two different databases (one for data flow diagrams, the other for state transition diagrams) and managed to get them out of synch all by myself. Can you imagine the problems with teams of 10 or more people trying to do that? It's a nightmare.

Sixth, I think it's essential for the toolset to have a simulation capability, preferably integrated with the diagrams. You can use a variety of simulation tools that require you to redraw the diagram in their particular form, but how do you know it's the same diagram? Chances are that it isn't.

The seventh criterion on my list is the facility to export data and products. I'm always looking at new tools that can supplement the ones I use, so having the ability to create an export file, in some simple ASCII format is essential. I also want the capability to migrate the data to other database tools when necessary, particularly if one becomes obsolete. Most tools use XML for the export file structure which really simplifies the process. Products from the tool need to be importable into the Microsoft Office suite for publication (and most do this well.)

The eighth item is to enable flexible reconfiguration. This means that I can view different elements by different names or limit the number of elements I want to see at one time. This feature lets me tailor the look and feel of the tool to meet specific customer needs.

The ninth criterion is that the tool can be applied to multiple lifecycle phases. I work across the lifecycle, sometimes doing architectures, sometimes detailed design, sometimes test and evaluation, and even operations and support. I want a tool set that can go with me.

The last item on the list is support for multiple disciplines. Like the lifecycle, I want to be capable of capturing program management data, configurations management, risk, quality, and other processes. My tool set must help this process.

In the end, you need your own criteria. When you come up with a set, conduct a trade study, like the one shown in Figure 5-29.

Criteria	DOORS/SA	CORE	Rational Rose
Supports your chosen methodology	IDEF	MBSE	UML
Provides several integrated functions	Yes	Yes	Yes (software focused)
Employs rule-based standards	Yes	Yes	Yes
Enforces consistency	Yes	Yes	Yes
Uses an integrated, common database	No	Yes	Yes
Permits simulation capability	No (except when adding a third tool)	Yes	Yes (with software coding)
Facilitates exporting data and products	Yes (but limited)	Yes	Yes
Enables flexible reconfiguration	Yes (but limited to "User Properties file)	Yes (using built-in schema extender)	No?
Applies to multiple lifecycle phases	Yes	Yes	No?
Supports multiple disciplines	No (Architecture focused)	Yes (Architecture to Software, CM, T&E)	No (software focused)

Figure 5-29. Build your own assessment of the tools.

I believe DOORS has support for at least pm - possibly others

So now we have a technique and tool, what's left? Process.

5.3 What Process Should We Use to Build Architectures and Designs?

In the beginning of Chapter 4, we introduced the DoDAF's 6-step architecture development process. In the Deskbook, this process is expanded as shown in Figure 5-30.[18]

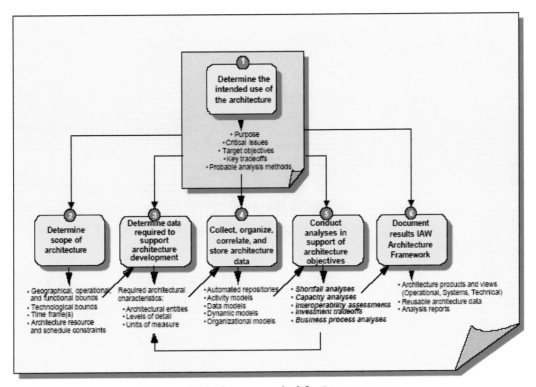

Figure 5-30. An expanded 6-step process.

This process provides a bit more detail and includes a feedback loop from step 5 back to 3, which we think is very important to recognize the iterative nature of these analyses. This diagram still doesn't help us too much, because we need to have processes for generating the models and analyses. So to develop an architecture, we need more detail (more steps) a clear timeline, and a process tailored to the technique and tool selected.

But before we delve too deep into process, we need to place the process in context with the lifecycle.

5.3.1 What Lifecycle Model Should We Use?

The DoD lifecycle model comes from the DoD 5000 series and is shown in Figure 5-31. This lifecycle model shows the various stages for development, with gates (milestones) shown as the letters: A, B, C.

There are many ways to implement and depict the lifecycle model. These implementation approaches include: spiral, where you re-look at the requirements and spiral through to create mature products at each

---

[18] DoD Architecture Framework v. 1.0, 9 February 2004, Deskbook, p. 2-2

spiral; incremental, where you define a design and implement different parts at different times (we used to call this pre-planned product improvement – P3I); prototyping, where we may drive forward a certain portion of the architecture to investigate high-risk, high payoff solutions; and finally COTS, where we decompose down to the level you can identify the COTS products, but must continue the process for the glue code or any database work, such as schema development.

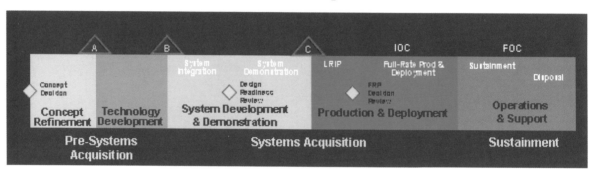

Figure 5-31. DoD's Lifecycle Model.

We also can depict these implementation approaches with the "V" diagram.[19] The "V" (see Figure 5-32) adds a visual cue that reminds the developer that the decomposition process is key to solving the problem. It also reminds us of what we have to do coming back up the "V" to bring it back into the on-going operations and support world.

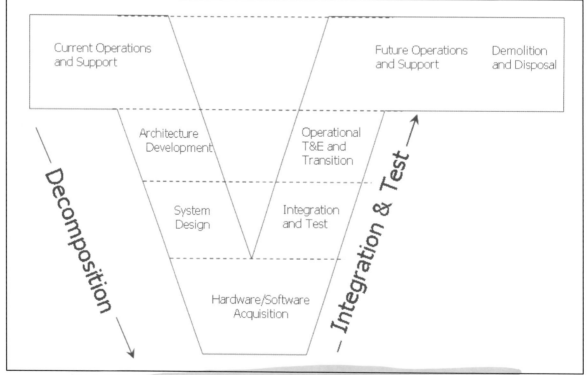

Figure 5-32. The "V" lifecycle model adds the concepts of decomposition and integration.

---

[19] The "V" diagram was originally developed by the Center for Systems Management. I highly recommend visiting their website at www.csm.com.

One of the things the "V" reminds us of is that we need to generate the verification and validation (or test and evaluation) requirements for the level opposite. For example, the architects should be generating the test requirements for the operational test and evaluation (OT&E). Similarly, the system design phase should provide the developmental test and evaluation requirements (DT&E).

The "V" diagram also includes the phase of demolition and disposal, a step often forgotten. With environmental impacts and unexploded munitions problems from WW I and II still with us, we should always remember this problem and consider it as part of the solution. It also should be considered integral to the transition planning; you will likely have to dispose of old equipment and software when transitioning to O&S.

Now that we have the big picture, let's look at the processes that support the architecture development.

5.3.2 What Processes Work?

Figures 5-33 shows the "V" again, but notice how I have shown a process at each level of decomposition. In fact, this is the name process at each level. That process contains the classical 4-stpe process used in system engineering for decades.[20]

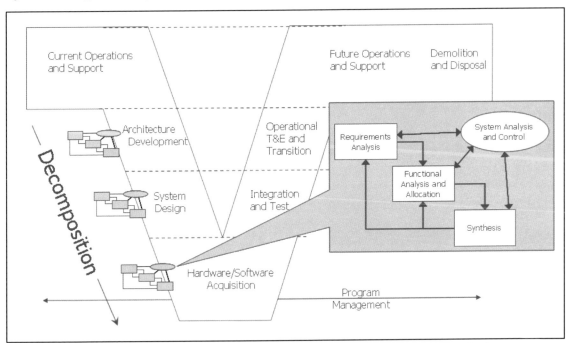

Figure 5-33. We can reuse the same process at each level of decomposition!

The four steps are: 1) requirements analysis, where you analyze the requirements provided by the customer and decompose them into

---

[20] This process was first characterized in MIL-STD-499B (draft), which was never published. It was subsequently adopted in EIA-632 and can be seen in the Defense Systems Management College "System Engineering Fundamentals" course (2001), p 6.

testable, requirements for development; 2) functional analysis and allocation, where you develop an understanding of the functional behavior of the system (or systems in the case of an architecture) and then allocate functions to performing components; 3) synthesis, where you develop the physical solution (i.e., define the components and interfaces); and 4) systems analysis and control, where you balance the three other analyses with trade-off studies, risk analysis, and other design verification and validation techniques.

I've successfully applied this process all throughout the decomposition portion of the lifecycle, because I early on recognized the versatility of this process and defined it in further detail (originally for a series of proposals).

If we expand this process (to a more readable size) as shown in Figure 5-34, we can see why this process works in a variety of lifecycle activities.

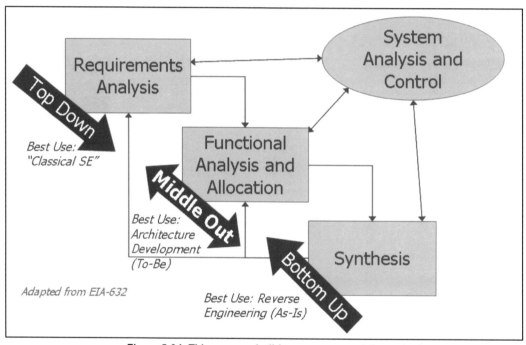

Figure 5-34. This process builds on a commercial standard.

Most people read this diagram as a "waterfall" chart, where you start with requirements analysis, then conduct functional analysis and allocation and finally synthesize a solution (or set of potential solutions). This "top-down" approach forms the basis for classical system engineering. But notice the two-way arrows on the chart. They indicate feedback loops. In fact, if you look at many of the formulations of this diagram, they don't show you where to start. So, I recognized that I can use this same process for reverse engineering, which is the basis for structured analysis's 4-step process and a good way to address the "as-is" architecture. But what do you do when your real goal is to develop a "to-be" or vision architecture? What happens when you aren't given a detailed set of requirements to start with?

That's when you want to work "middle-out." The requirements you receive can be very broad, yet fuzzy. For example, when I was asked to help develop the "Vision Architecture for Airborne Reconnaissance," I was told to make it Joint Vision 2010 compatible. I went to this wonderful strategy documents and found the one sentence on airborne reconnaissance. I had full traceability to my requirements at that point, but it didn't help much. I needed more.

Fortunately, I had been working a number of Advanced Concept Technology Demonstrations (ACTD) before this and had formulated the middle-out approach to developing a system of systems. An updated version of that process is shown in Figure 5-35.

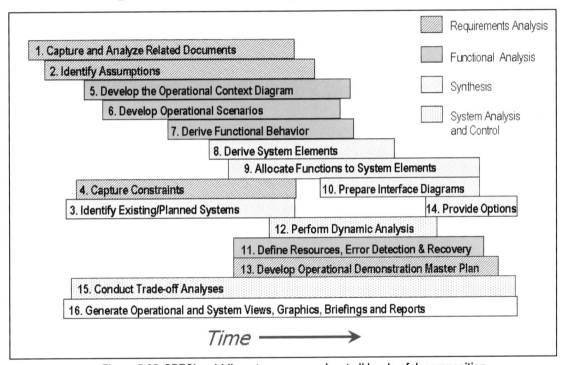

Figure 5-35. SPEC's middle-out process works at all levels of decomposition.

This figure shows my process in a compact timeline format. The steps are numbered to indicate their nominal start sequence. Notice that most of these steps overlap, which demonstrates the concurrent, iterative nature of this process. My process goes slightly beyond the minimum requirements for developing DoDAF products, since it assumes that this process is not an end in itself. It provides the necessary information for executing the resulting architecture, including the requirements analysis and operational demonstration.

Now let's go through each of the steps, so that it will become clear how they work.

Step 1: *Capture and Analyze Related Documents.* First we obtain any related documents, capture them in the architecture repository (CORE or the AV-2), and analyze them to identify issues, risks, and assumptions for other activities and capabilities.

Step 2: *Identify Assumptions*. We identify the assumptions made in Step 1 and review those assumptions with the Government to ensure that subsequent steps in this process meet project objectives. You should capture these assumption and decisions in your tool of choice (in my case CORE) and document them in the AV-1.

Step 3: *Identify Existing and Planned Systems*. Of course, I hate to reinvent the wheel, so I recommend conducting a survey of the current and on-going activities related to this architecture to ensure that capabilities already available or planned are taken into account in this architecture. This step reduces the possibility for unnecessary duplication of effort. Coordination and monitoring of the progress of planned systems must also be included in this step. Planned systems that are incorporated as part of the architecture should be included in a SV-8 and/or SV-9 diagrams to enhance transition planning.

Step 4: *Capture Constraints*. In this step, we capture the technical, schedule, and political constraints imposed by external laws, policies, regulations, and standards. These constraints often come from the previous three steps, as well as later analyses. This step results in the development of the technical standards views (TV-1 and TV-2).

Step 5: *Develop Operational Context Diagram*. The operational context diagram is an extension of the classical context diagram used in system engineering. I extended it to include interactions between external systems. It describes the overall architecture environment, including interactions between stakeholders, external systems/architectures, facilities, and resources. The operational context diagram shall form the basis for the OV-1, OV-2 and SV-1 DoDAF products. We will discuss this diagram in more depth in the next subsection.

Step 6: *Develop Operational Scenarios*. In this step, we develop a set of operational scenarios that represent the scope of potential uses of the "As-Is" architecture. Some people call these use cases or threads. I've found that building a set of scenarios from the simplest case to the most complex and reusing activities/functions as appropriate provide an effective way to create a concept of operations (CONOPS) at a reasonable size. These scenarios represent typical user and system processes. The results of this step provide the initial OV-5/OV-6c and SV-4/SV-10c products. These scenarios can also form the basis for the test scenarios in the Operational Demonstration Master Plan (ODMP).

Step 7: *Derive Functional Behavior*. Here we derive the overall functional behavior from the individual scenarios developed as part of Step 6. If you are clever in selecting the set of scenarios so that they build one upon the other, instead of coming up with a dissimilar, but overlapping set, you will find this task to be much easier. The results of this step provide the final OV-5/OV-6c and SV-4/SV-10c products.

Step 8: *Derive System Elements*. In this step, we derive the system elements from the functional behavior (really just packaging the functionality) and potential COTS, GOTS, and legacy systems. We create

142

components that provide as simple as possible interfaces between system elements. The outcome of this task results in the final SV-1.

Step 9: *Allocate Functions to System Elements*. Obviously this step goes hand-in-hand with Steps 7 and 8. Here we allocate functions to system elements, which establishes the traceability between the functional behavior and the system elements. You can also use this step to distinguish between operational activities and system functions (if you must.)

Step 10: *Prepare Interface Diagrams*. This step continues the allocation process, ensuring that we've documented what data elements flow though which interfaces. Most of this becomes obvious when we complete Step 9, as the functional allocation to system elements defines the data that must flow between the elements. "All" that's left is to determine the mechanism for the data transmissions and creating the resulting diagrams. Here's where we finalize the OV-3 and SV-6.

Step 11: *Define Resources, Error Detection, and Recovery Processes*. As part of the scenario development and functional behavior analysis, we need to include the effects of non-ideal processes, where errors and other alternatives are detected as part of the process and corrected. In addition, the use of any resources, such as personnel, computers, etc. will be included in the functional analysis developed under Steps 6 & 7.

Step 12: *Perform Dynamic Analyses*. Just like in Step 11, we need to perform dynamic analyses of the individual scenarios, the overall functional behavior, and the overall behavior as constrained by the physical architecture, including the interface capacities and latencies. So clearly, this step must be performed concurrently with Steps 6, 7, and 9 to develop an executable architecture. You can also document the results of this analysis in the *Findings* section of the AV-1.

Step 13: *Develop Operational Demonstration Master Plan*. I think it's critical that as part of the architecture development process, we create a draft of the operational demonstration master plan (ODMP) or Test and Evaluation Master Plan (TEMP). The purpose of this document is to enable the future acceptance testing of the resulting architecture design and to demonstrate potential issues and problems that will require resolution in the architecture. You should include people who know test and evaluation processes and capabilities as part of your team in developing this document.

Step 14: *Provide Options*: It's important to realize that you aren't creating an architecture just for the fun of it. All along the way, you will identify any potential problems (shortfalls or gaps) with the "As-Is" architecture and provide options for resolution of these problems. Plan on creating a briefing that summarizes these options, even if they have been decided along the way, and incorporate them in the *Findings* section of the AV-1.

Step 15: *Conduct Trade-off Analyses*. Clearly, all through this process, you will need to perform trade-off analyses, using stakeholder validated evaluation criteria, to derive requirements, select scenarios, select components, including COTS and GOTS, and other potential options. Summarize these as part of the options (Step 14) at the end of the process and present them to the customer. You can also document these trade-off analyses in the *Findings* section of the AV-1.

Step 16: *Generate Views, Briefings, and Reports.* This last step recognizes that throughout any architecture project, you will have to produce reports and briefings to show status and progress. By using the technique and tools selected (particularly CORE), I have found that the development of reports and briefings is now a simple by-product of the process, instead of being a driver.

Figure 5-36 summarizes the production of DoDAF products throughout the process. As you can see, I recommend delivering an early draft of the AV-1 at the beginning of the project, so that it starts off well. Final versions of the products are shown at roughly the time they should be finished and associated with the steps that produce them.

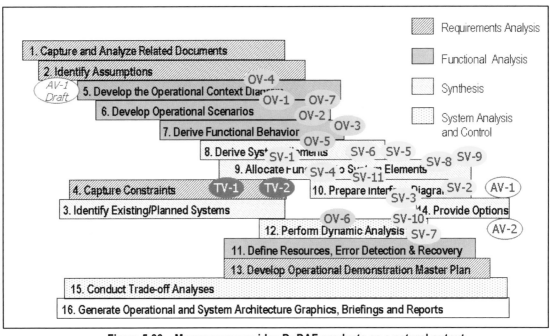

Figure 5-36. My process provides DoDAF products as a natural output.

You can repeat this process in layers, for each level of decomposition, assuming roughly 3-4 levels per major "V" area (architecture, system design, and acquisition). By taking this approach, you can create a number of architecture deliveries, based on a complete pass through the process. Vitech, the makers of CORE, call this the "Onion Model." If applied correctly,[21] you can converge on a solution.

---

[21] One of the Onion Model rules is that you can not make changes at a low level only. You must go back up at each higher level in sequence and make the changes there as well. This rule enforces convergence.

144

Now that we have the overall process, let's talk about how we get started by developing the operational context diagram.

5.3.3 How Do We Start?

The classical system engineering context diagram is shown in Figure 5-37. External systems provide inputs and outputs through external interfaces. Inside the system, we break it down into components with their internal interfaces. Once we establish this system boundary, we ignore the outside world. However, I found that in architecture development ignorance is not bliss.

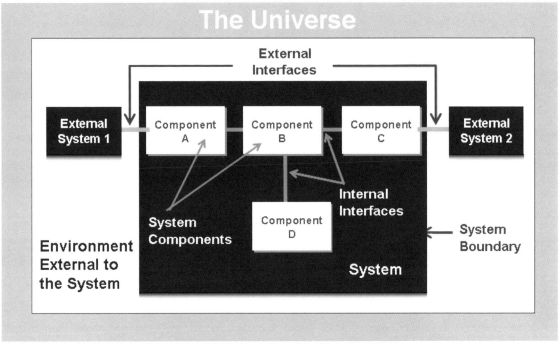

Figure 5-37. The classical SE context diagram limits the architecture study.

The Operational Context Diagram also describes the scope of the architecture, but it includes the *key interfaces between the external architectures/systems*, as well as the interfaces between the external systems and the architecture under development. This difference allows you to make dramatic changes in the architecture, thus providing a means to transform from the As-Is architecture to the To-Be.

For example, when we were developing the Vision Architecture for Airborne Reconnaissance, we were told to "get out-of-the-box." So we created the series of diagrams shown in Figure 5-38. The Today (circa 1996) and Transition diagrams (estimated early 2000) include both satellite and airborne reconnaissance capabilities. We showed that our "competition" was also providing direct information to users, who we named *information consumers*, since it wasn't just warfighters who used our products and services. These first two diagrams enable us to realize that our consumers would be getting products and services from other Government organizations and commercial companies. As such, we recognized the problem required a new way to select services and distribute products to the consumers. Since the concepts of net-centricity and even the Internet were new, we saw that what was needed was some sort of Internet-like global information interchange to allow the consumers to access not only raw products and services, but also derivative products from *value added resellers*, which included intelligence analysts. The vast number of products and services, particularly in the commercial world, we were growing exponentially, so we also recognized the need for information brokers, much like the service Google and the Drudge Report provide today.

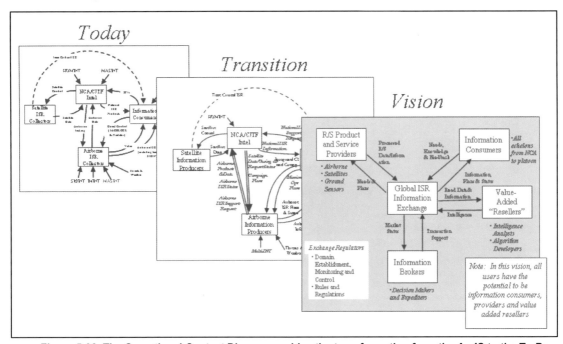

Figure 5-38. The Operational Context Diagram enables the transformation form the As-IS to the To-Be.

So, as you can see, by including the interaction between the satellite capabilities and the customer, we were able to subsume their architecture into ours, creating a new way to look at and solve problems. I've applied this same technique to other architectures and found it to be equally beneficial.

Another feature of the operational context diagram comes from being able to derive several DoDAF products for it. As you can see from the diagram, it is already very close to an OV-2. The only thing missing is the operational activities, which would make the diagram too busy. You can also create an OV-1 by replacing the boxes with icons. If we include physical linkages and systems, this diagram can also form the basis for the SV-1. So again our methodology results in a number of DoDAF products from a single diagram. That makes life much simpler.

Now that we've seen the top levels, perhaps it would be good to look at the overall process in more depth. This next subsection does that for requirements analysis, functional analysis and allocation, synthesis, and systems analysis and control.

5.3.4 How Can We Develop a Detailed Architecture?

The *requirements analysis* process, Figure 5-39, shows how we take the original requirement statements from users and other sources, decompose them into individual requirements, identify critical issues, ensure that the requirement can be tested, identify and mitigate any associated risks, and review the requirements with the customer and users. The result is an architecture requirements database that contains the working requirements (prior to validation by the customer). Once the requirements have been validated, you can include that information in the database. Any of the working requirements not validated can be kept within this database along with the reason they were not included, thus avoiding duplication of later efforts. You will find this avoids the *throwing the baby out with the bath water* syndrome when new management takes over the project.

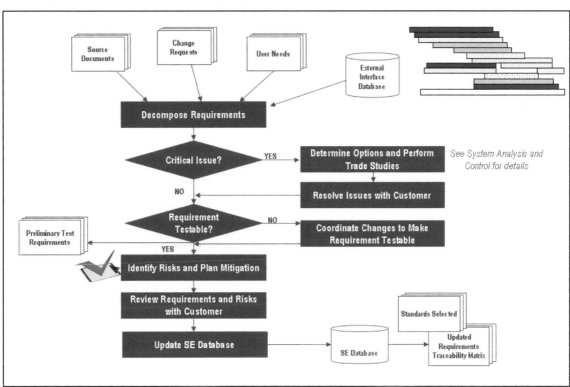

Figure 5-39. Requirements analysis captures and understands the customer's needs.

The key to requirements analysis is the development of requirements that are: 1) Correct, i.e. they describe the user's true intent and are legally possible; 2) Complete, i.e. express a whole, single idea, and not portions of one or many; 3) Clear, i.e., unambiguous and not confusing to any reader; 4) Consistent, i.e., not in conflict with other requirements; 5) Verifiable, i.e., provable within realistic cost and schedule that the architecture meets the requirement; 6) Traceable, i.e., uniquely identified, and able to be tracked to predecessor and successor lifecycle items/objects, such as functions or components; 7) Feasible, i.e., able to be implemented with existing or projected technology, and within cost and schedule; 8) Modular, i.e., can be changed without excessive impact on other requirements; and 9) Design, i.e., does not impose a specific solution on design ("what" not "how").

In the development of these good requirements, you may want to avoid the following pitfalls:

- DON'T use ambiguous language
- DON'T use bullet lists; use numbered lists instead
- DON'T use jargon
- DON'T use language that provides an escape clause; .e.g, "The user shall be able to access the Internet as often as is practicable"
- DON'T write long, rambling sentences
- DON'T put two requirements in one sentence; e.g., "The system shall ... and ..."
- DON'T use vague terms; e.g., "user-friendly"
- DON'T include suggestions or possibilities; e.g., "may", "should", "ought"
- DON'T include wishful thinking; e.g., "The system shall be 100% reliable"

As you can see, requirements analysis is as much of an art as it is a science. The rules of thumb should help you create a better set of specifications in your ICD, CDD, and CPD products.

The next process (see Figure 5-40), *functional analysis and allocation*, develops the context for the use of architecture, develops use case analyses, examines operational options and tradeoffs, updates the system behavior model that integrates these use cases, analyzes that model to ensure that it is executable, identifies, and mitigates any risks surfaced by this analysis and presents the results to the customer for approval. Once the segments and items have been identified (during the first steps of the Synthesis Solution process), the functions developed during the use case analysis are allocated to particular items. Thus, iteration between these two processes will likely occur to optimize the solution.

One of the key concepts for this process is my strategy for scenario development. I start with the simplest scenario that the team and I can dream up, then, we think of the most difficult scenario. These two scenarios form the bounds that we want to work within. Then we define another 5-7 scenarios that will build, one on the other from the simplest to the most difficult. We then create executable, enhanced function flow block diagrams (EFFBD) for each scenario, reusing functions from the previous scenarios. *This set of scenarios can be the basis for your operational concept and operational demonstration master plan.*

If you use this approach, you may already have an integrated behavior diagram; however, it may be too big to communicate well. You can abstract it up to the context diagram level, building each level of "decomposition" as you go. Make sure that once you have the operational behavior, you continue the decomposition process until you can identify the functions needed for the components. You can use the scenarios you developed to verify that this integrated behavior still works for those specific cases. You should also make sure that the diagrams execute using a discrete event simulation.

Allocation is the simple mapping of functions to components and items to links. You can determine best ways to "package" functions into components to minimize the interface requirements (i.e. data flows) between components.

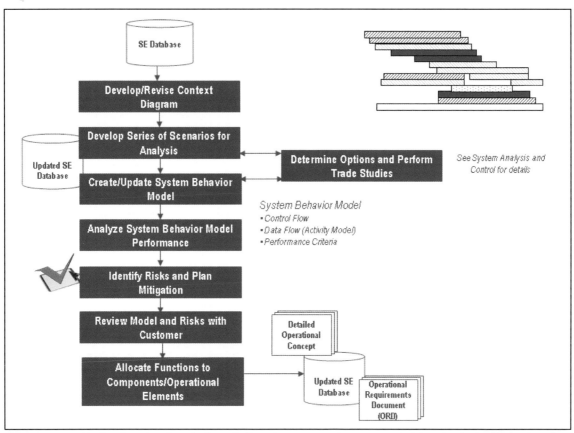

Figure 5-40. Our functional analysis and allocation process focuses on deriving the desired behavior of the architecture.

Synthesis (see Figure 5-41) begins with the identification of the segments or configuration items that may require modification, enhancement, or replacement. These segments and items may include current corporate services when they have been determined to be ready for integration into the baseline. With the extensive use of COTS, you may have to replace software that has been changed significantly in a new version or discontinued by a particular vendor. You will want to coordinate all replacements with the customer, as soon as they have been identified. If items require new designs, "glue code" or scripts, I usually apply state-of-the-technology design tools, such as CORE, to ensure that the design meets quality standards. As with the other processes, I like to identify risks early and develop mitigation approaches, prior to review with the customer. Most customer don't want problems ... they're paying you for solutions. Remember to try to give them choices along the way. Once designs and COTS/GOTS product selections and specifications have been approved by the customer, you can support the implementation of the acquisition plan by the customer, as well.

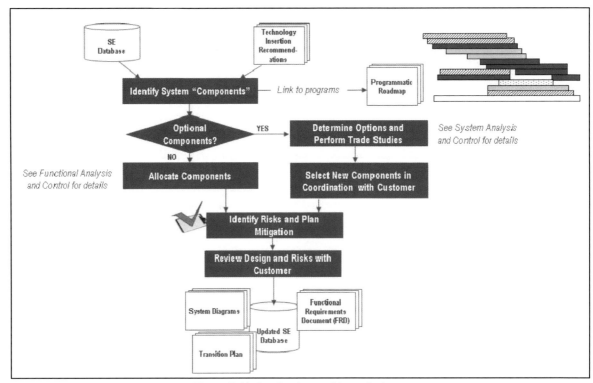

Figure 5-41. Synthesis provides solutions.

The synthesis process can also help you define when to stop decomposition. In today's COTS/GOTS/Legacy world, we don't want to reinvent things. When you can identify potential products or at least classes of products, you're done. You can write the design specification that the system designers can use to develop the systems of the architecture. What you need to be careful is to remember what make a good requirement. Make sure you don't over specify (or specify a particular solution). If necessary, roll back up a level if it looks like you have decomposed too low. Make sure you use "functional" wording to avoid over specification. Also define end-to-end performance factors, not detailed ones for each component. If you follow these simple rules, you will end up with a much more robust architecture.

The last of the four processes (see Figure 5-42), *systems analysis and control,* is used throughout the preceding three processes. This process includes: the assessment of new technologies; requirements and options to determine what ones should be included in the analysis; the development of metrics to control the trade studies; the analysis of the effectiveness; the use of O&M, security and training impacts of the options; risk analysis, performance and cost analyses; and the

150

recommended changes. By applying this process and documenting the results of the tradeoff, we enhance the quality of the other design-related processes.

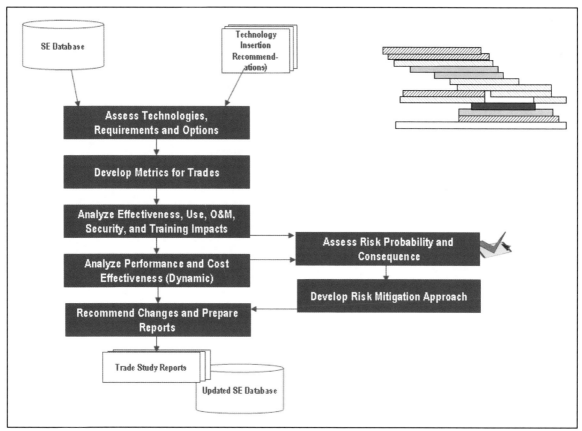

Figure 5-42. Systems analysis and control keeps your architecture project balanced.

Recognize that you may conduct a variety of trade-off analysis for each of the other processes. For example, if you're conducting requirements analysis, you may want to consider alternative derived requirements, alternative standards, and alternative sets of performance criteria. In functional analysis and allocation, create alternative scenarios and allocations. For synthesis, make sure you provide alternative solutions and packaging. The key to conducting these analyses is to not *just do them in your head; document them as you go.*

In summary, we need to consider how to define and implement these processes. Start with someone's "off-the-shelf" process, determine how it needs to be tailored (minimally to not at all, if possible.) Make sure you tailor it to the toolset and technique. Publish the process making sure it is a "must read" for all personnel working on the architecture development. You may want to develop or use vendor training courses. And make sure that process monitoring is part of your quality management activity.

5.4 What Else Do We Need?

The last part of developing a methodology is to determine who should be part of the architecture development team. First, you need someone with vision. This person can project to the future needs and state of technology. Crystal balls are not necessary, but would help. You also need someone who can perform the detailed system engineering. As we've demonstrated in the rest of this chapter, system engineering skills form the basis for the technique and process.

You will also want to have someone who understands each of the relevant domains. This group of subject matter experts can also include test and evaluation personnel and other specialty engineering disciplines.

Finally, you clearly need someone familiar with the process, technique, and tools. Consider vendor training if necessary. Make sure you have everyone training in the processes and procedures that you will use and make sure they know the techniques at an expert level.

As you can ascertain by this list, one person can not do this job. You will need a team. Their pooled expertise will reduces program risk and improve the architecture products.

In the next chapter, we will take the methodology presented here and apply it to a sample problem of interest. If you're a little confused now, I think you will find it very helpful.

6

How Does SE Provide the Architecture Views?

In this chapter, I will take a concrete example I developed and use the steps in the process that was shown in the previous chapter. I will use the CORE tool and technique from Model-Based System Engineering (MBSE) to create the integrated architecture views. As a result, you will see how we develop and use the executable architecture to communicate results to decision-makers; so they can investment strategy decisions, portfolio management, and system design decisions.

The example comes from a problem we've been dealing with for some time – Time Sensitive Targets (TSTs), which we used to call time critical targets (among other things.) I always wondered how good an example this was, until I was at an architecture conference in Tidewater, Virginia. An Army Major General who had recently returned from Iraq, not long after the "Shock and Awe" campaign told a story about dealing with TSTs that sounded eerily like this sample problem.

A number of classes I've taught have addressed this problem or ones like it, and we get an amazingly different set of answers, even with my facilitation. So, it goes to show that there is no single, right answer. If you give a problem to two different groups, you will get two different answers. However with the DoDAF and a little more, we can compare the two answers and see how they differ, how they overlap, and which might provide the best solution.

Problem: Develop a System of Systems Architecture (SOSA) for Time Sensitive Targets

The objective of this sample problem is to develop a systems-of-system architecture for responding to the threat of mobile missile launcher systems using a new tactical UAV. We can assume for this problem that a new agency was formed (Advanced Airborne Reconnaissance Agency – AARA ... after all it's only a matter of time before someone reinvents DARO). AARA is responsible for the development of this new tactical UAV (Little Eye) and wants to develop an architecture that captures the usefulness of this new capability. The capability needs and potential assets for this architecture study are provided below.

1. This architecture shall:

   1.1 Publish raw and processed data from a new tactical UAV to support operations spanning the Joint Task Force to Platoon levels;

   1.2 Platoons may laser designate targets of interest;

   1.3 Discovery of information must respond, within a few minutes of the request, preferably within seconds of most requests for all responsive forces; and

   1.4 Strike aircraft will receive subscribed data on TST from Airborne Communications Node (ACN) UAVs

2. Architecture will include the following assets:

   2.1 F-18 Navy Strike Aircraft for TST attack;

   2.2 Special Forces platoon for laser designation task;

   2.3 Global Hawk ACN;

   2.4 New UAV (Little Eye) for electro-optical/infrared sensing of the launch flash;

   2.5 Upgraded Patriot system, with an upgraded ground-based radar and exhaust seeker warhead; and

   2.6 Joint Command and Control system using Net-Centric Enterprise Services.

(handwritten margin note: not exactly the best grammar...)

(handwritten note above 2.4: EO/IR sensing ...)

Needless to say, I tried to make sure every service was represented in this statement; and as many interests as possible, including some new and emerging capabilities.

When I originally developed this problem, a number of the students felt that they needed more information, and so I created the "interface specification" below. I actually thought they overly constrain the problem and make it a near term "to-be" architecture, but let's use it as well.

Interface Specification for New Tactical UAV (LITTLE EYE)
From the Advanced Airborne Reconnaissance Agency

1) LITTLE EYE has a single imaging sensor (digital camera providing video and still pictures)

2) LITTLE EYE uses the Common Data Link (CDL) protocol for providing communications between the aircraft and the ground Data Dissemination Element (DDE) at rates of 400 kBits/second

3) The DDE is connected to the Secure Wireless LAN used by the Brigade in the Field, operating at 1 Mbits/second

4) The Brigade uses satellite communications to link to higher headquarters to disseminate information

5) The Brigade uses standard audio communications systems to transmit information to lower echelons

Note: All names, organizations, and information above are fictitious and intended for the use in this example only.

To conduct this architecture study, we will use the process discussed in Chapter 5. It is repeated for your convenience in Figure 6-1 (it avoids having to turn back so many pages).

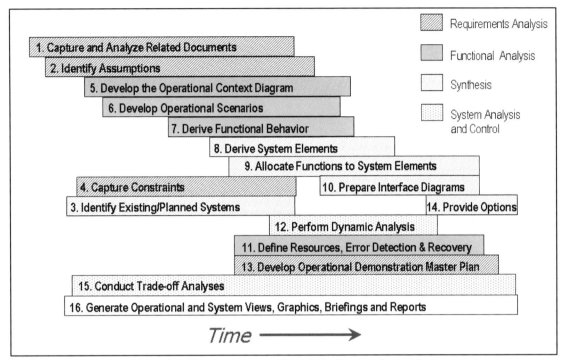

Figure 6-1. The process we will apply to the sample problem.

Now let's go through this process step by step using the sample problem and tool to show how we can develop an integrated, executable architecture. Please also note, as we go through this example, I have modified the CORE schema; so if you don't see this exact set of elements, relationships, and attributes out-of-the-box, don't worry. You can easily adjust the schema yourself or e-mail me at info@spec-1.com to request a copy of my schema.

Step 1: Capture and Analyze Related Documents

The first thing to do is import the problem statement and specification into CORE. CORE provides an "Element Extractor" tool that can read a number of different formats, including Microsoft Word documents. You can see this tool in Figure 6-2. In 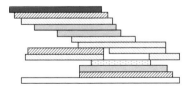 this figure, I show extracting the objective into an *Originating Requirement* class element. All the attributes of the class are provided once you select it from the list. You can also see all the potential relationships in this window. Notice how I've selected the "documented by" relationship. It's "target class" is a *Document*; in this case, it's the specification of the problem. You can adjust the attributes of this class as well by double-clicking on it and bringing up the "PropertySheet" for it (see Figure 6-3).

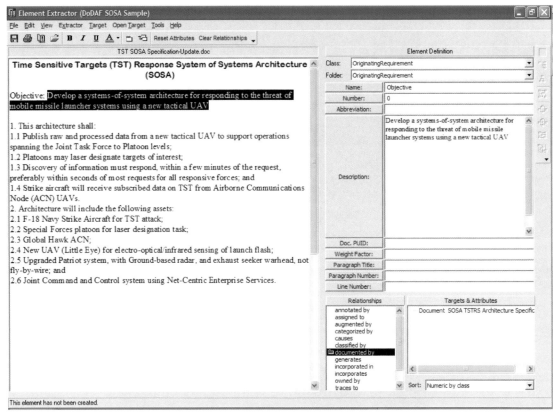

Figure 6-2. Extract and analyze requirements as you go.

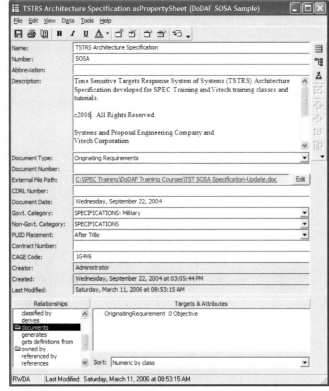

Figure 6-3. Keep track of your documents as well.

Note also how one of the attributes is *External File Path.* This attribute allows you to establish a hyperlink between the original document and this database element; so in this way, you can keep track of the documents you use without bloating the database.

If we follow this procedure for the remainder of the document, we end up with a set of high level requirements. But how do we analyze these requirements and get them so that we can gain a better understanding of what the customer really wants?

MBSE and CORE provide several other classes to capture information related to the *OriginatingRequirement* elements. One of these classes is the *Issue.* Issues capture information about potential problems or concerns or just things you want to resolve before proceeding with other analysis processes. For example, if you look at the statement provided in requirement 1.1, it states "they may receive raw and processed data." What does that mean? What's raw data and what's processed data? How are they different? Figure 6-4 shows this Issue and the attributes.

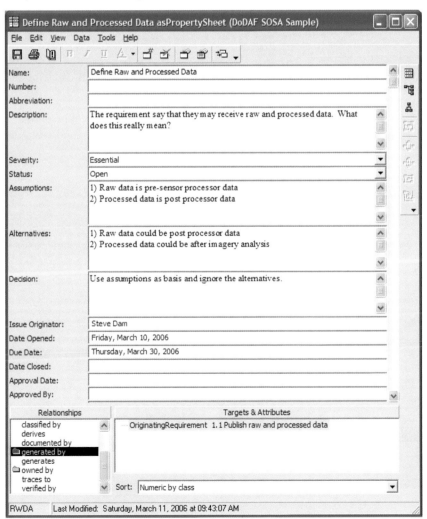

Figure 6-4. Capturing issues documents the decision process.

You can see that it gives you space to capture assumptions, alternatives, decisions, and who made the decision and when. You can manage your project just with this feature. Imagine capturing these as you go (since any element can generate an *Issue*) and presenting them to your customer on a weekly basis for a decision. It should help your customer interaction tremendously.

Another consideration during the requirements analysis is the identification of the key performance parameters (KPPs). This piece of information was so important that I added an element called *Key Performance Parameter* to the CORE schema (they already had a class called *PerformanceIndex*, but I wanted to separate the KPPs out at the element level – you could do the same thing by either aliasing the *PerformanceIndex* name or create a *Category* called KPP and associate the KPPs with it). I identified two: Probability of Kill and Time-to-Target. Figure 6-5 shows the *PropertySheet* for the Probability of Kill KPP.

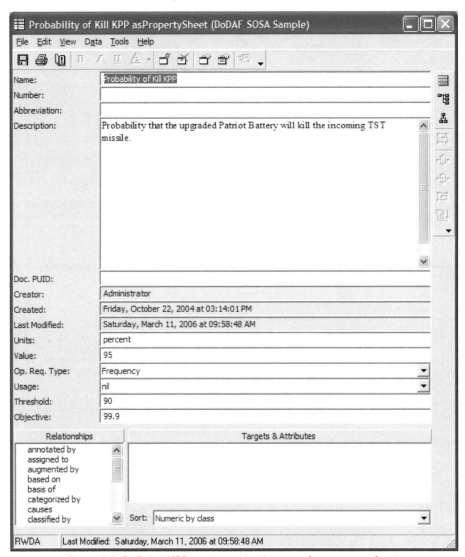

Figure 6-5. Defining KPPs puts emphasis on performance up front.

You will want to repeat this step for any relevant documents, including the Little Eye and other specifications, concepts of operations, standards, etc. As you can see by the timeline, you can (and will) be adding information as you go. You will discover the need or the existence of other documents. Use this step as much as needed to capture the information you require to get the job done.

Step 2: Identify Assumptions

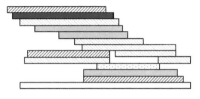

We saw in the previous step the place where MBSE and CORE capture assumptions. Assumptions should really be associated with issues, so I have never changed this. However, if you think they should be their own class of elements, you can easily add them to your schema.

The most important thing to do is get your customer to agree and validate any issues and assumptions. Using this feature of the tool, with the weekly report, enables you to make your customer "party to the crime." They will feel ownership and help defend your project. They will also see steady progress, without interfering with the production.

Step 3: Identify Existing/Planned Systems

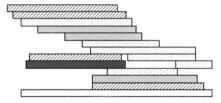

In this step, we first want to identify what systems currently exist that may affect this architecture. You might call this the "as-is" architecture, but that's too broad for this step alone. Here we just list the systems that we need to interact with. You can start with the problem statement. It lists a couple of current systems: the Navy F-18, and laser designators. The others (Global Hawk CAN, Little Eye, Upgraded Patriot and JC2) are systems under development (theoretically) and thus fall into the planned category. The interface specification also includes a planned system, the Secure Wireless Local Area Network (LAN).

You can capture all of these in the *Component* class. This class is designed as a place for the information on physical systems you want to include in the architecture. You may also decide to capture more generic versions of these systems (e.g. strike aircraft instead of F-18) as *OperationalElement* objects. Then you can include the Platoon, Brigade, and other operational nodes for your generic systems.

Also with the planned systems, you will want to capture the time they will become available. You can do this as a *Category* or add an attribute to collect this information. It's up to you.

Step 4: Capture Constraints

Constraints are a special class of requirements. Constraints can be operational (requires 24x7 coverage), physical ("paint it gray" for the Navy), or standards (CDL – Common Data Link standard for Airborne Reconnaissance platforms referenced in the sample problem) based. MBSE and CORE provide for these different types of constraints with either separate classes (in the pre-5.1 version DoDAF schema) or attributes on a general Requirement class (5.1 and later versions).

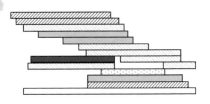

Since we want to generate TV-1 and TV-2 products, we are especially interested in the standards. I include both operational and technical standards in my analyses. In this sample problem, operational standards, such as Joint Tactics, Techniques, and Procedures (JTTP), provide an important basis for how the operations will be conducted. Obviously, we would want to include the technical standards from the Joint Technical Architecture (JTA), including the DISR On-line.

Figure 6-6 shows an example for this sample problem of the CDL. Note how we have shown its relationship to a physical link, which we define in a later step.

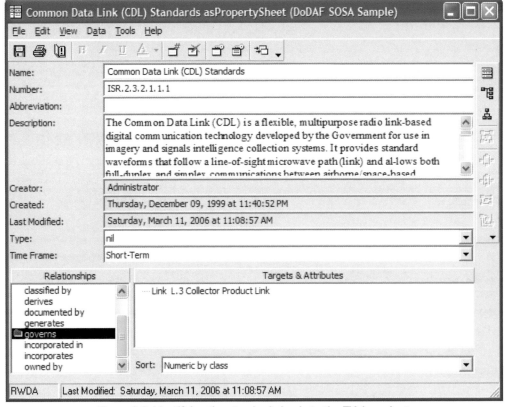

Figure 6-6. Identifying the standards leads to the TV-1 product.

Another set of constraints to consider is the laws and policies that govern the development, operations, and support. We need to remember that many peacetime laws, especially environmental laws, when we use the systems during testing and training. Some of these constraints might be ignored during a war, but even those come back to haunt the Department. We're still cleaning up toxic chemicals from World War I in D.C. and unexploded munitions in housing developments across the country.

One of the most important to consider at all times is the frequency standards. With the overcrowding of telecom these days, frequency selection becomes a critical factor. You can imagine interference problems occurring in peacetime operations such as training, emergency operations, like disaster relief, and warfighting operations, like those in Iraq and Afghanistan. Hence, constraints go beyond just standards and become a very important part of developing a complete architecture.

Step 5: Develop the Operational Context Diagram

Notice how early the next step in our process, the development of the operational context diagram (OCD), starts. I began this diagram in a couple of different ways. I sometimes just use a whiteboard or large sheet of paper and begin drawing the elements for the problem statement. 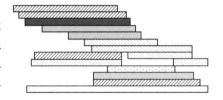 I can do the same thing in CORE using the physical block diagram. Use whatever makes the most sense at the time.

Figure 6-7 shows one of my OCDs in the most universal tool available: Microsoft PowerPoint. Notice that this diagram is just a bunch of boxes and lines. You don't have to be a great artist to produce this. The boxes represent the elements of the problem statement with one specific addition. The problem statement didn't mention a "C4ISR Management Systems," but my domain experts, and my experience at DARO, tell me that I need one. Of course, there are a number of existing systems I may want to consider using or modifying so I can use them. I also included the Global Information Grid (GIG), because I know I'll have to be compatible with it.

You would want to expand this diagram to include: the Patriot missile system; the SOF team using the laser designator (you can consider that part of the "platoon" box); and the new Joint Command and Control (JC2) System (which could be considered part of the GIG –the Net-Centric Enterprise Services are explicitly part of the GIG Architecture).

Now you can see this could also be a starting point for the OV-1, OV-2 and the SV-1. For example, the OV-1 would replace the boxes with icons, the link lines with lightning bolts and a cool background and we might have something like Figure 6-8. Notice the black lightning bolt. It represents a secure communications path.

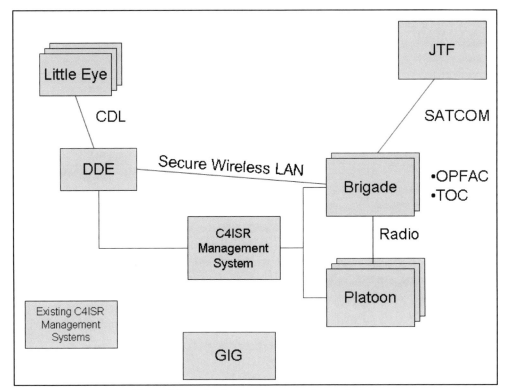

Figure 6-7. A simple drawing can get you started.

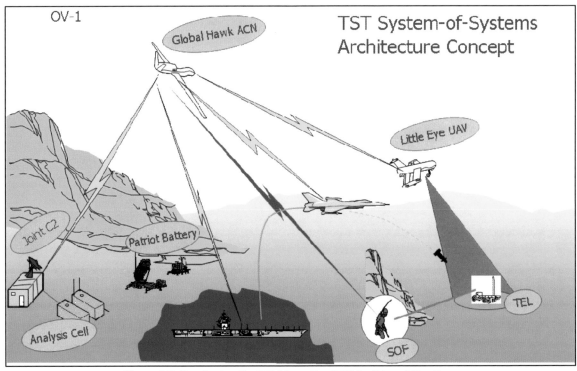

Figure 6-8. Developing the OV-1 from the OCD isn't too difficult.

We also would like to get our OV-2 and SV-1. For these diagrams, I used CORE's physical block diagram in two different classes: *OperationalElement* and *Component*. Figure 6-9 and 6-10 show these two diagrams.

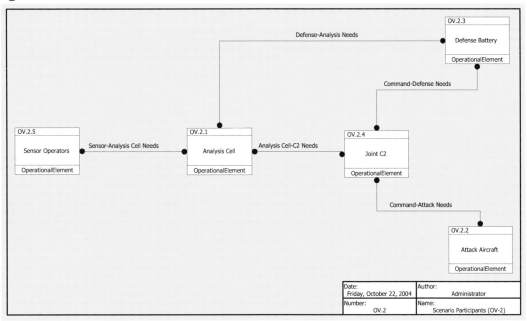

Figure 6-9. The OV-2 shows only the operational elements.

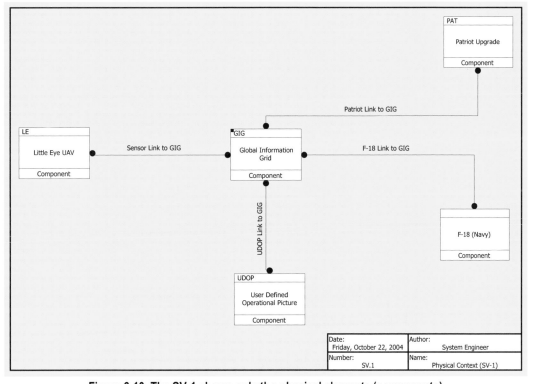

Figure 6-10. The SV-1 shows only the physical elements (components).

These diagrams introduce a few new ideas and systems. The OV-2 brings in the idea of an Analysis Cell to support the defense and attack operational elements. In the SV-1, I added the idea of the User Defined Operational Picture (UDOP), which is being developed to replace the Common Operational Picture (COP). You can easily get the domain experts to add this kind of information when you get a group together to draw the OCD. Don't constrain them. Let them add whatever makes sense and more if necessary. You can always weed out the things you don't want.

Notice again in just these few steps, we've generated a number of the integrated architecture products, including the parts of the AV-1 (Step 2), TV-1 (Step 4), OV-2 (Step 5), and SV-1 (Steps 3 & 5). By capturing this information in the database provided by CORE, we are building the AV-2 (as long as we are good architects and fill in those description fields for each of the objects we're defining.)

Also you may want to create a number of OV-1, OV-2, and SV-1 products from the specific scenarios discussed in the next step.

Step 6: Develop Operational Scenarios

One of the most difficult problems in developing an architecture is coming up with a reasonable number of scenarios to analyze. On one project I worked on, they defined hundreds of scenarios (before I got there). Analyzing and managing the overlap in these 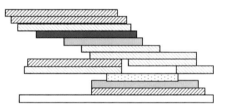 scenarios took an immense amount of time and effort. So how could they have avoided this problem? They could have applied what I usually do (when given the opportunity.) I construct a set of scenarios that build upon each other. For this problem, I decided that the simplest scenario I wanted to develop was where the system of systems architecture detects the missile launch, and then locates and kills the transporter-erector-launcher threat. Now you might come up with something simpler, but that's were I started. Then I asked myself, "What's the most difficult problem I want to address with this scenario?" I chose a scenario to "Find and Destroy Threats Theater-wide." This scenario will include: multiple targets and multiple defensive and offensive forces, finding and killing threats before and after launches, and various adverse environmental conditions. Then I defined 5 more scenarios that fit in between these extremes, building one upon the other. My list ended up being:

◆ Scenario 1: Detect, Locate and Kill TEL

◆ Scenario 2: Defend Against Missile Attack

◆ Scenario 3: Defense and Kill TEL (combines 1 & 2)

- Scenario 4: Find Threat Before Launch (adds new technologies)
- Scenario 5: Find and Destroy Threat Before Launch (combines results from 3 & 4)
- Scenario 6: Find and Destroy Multiple Threats (adds complexity of more than one sensor and threat)
- Scenario 7: Find and Destroy Threats Theater-wide (adds all the necessary assets and threats projected)

Now if I tried to build these independently, I would create overlapping operational activities/system functions to perform these missions. Plus, can you imagine the difficulty of starting with Scenario 7? I know that would be hard for me to get my head wrapped around. So we start with Scenario 1 and work our way up.

The EFFBD for Scenario 1 I developed is shown in Figure 6-11.

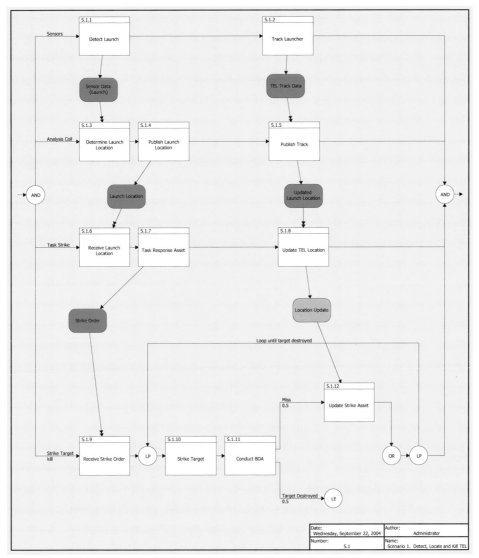

Figure 6-11. Scenario 1 EFFBD provides a starting point for functional analysis.

As you can see this diagram is fairly complex. It includes a number of features, including the publishing of launch location and track. In developing the EFFBD for Scenario 2, I reused some of those same functions (operational activities), as shown in Figure 6-12.

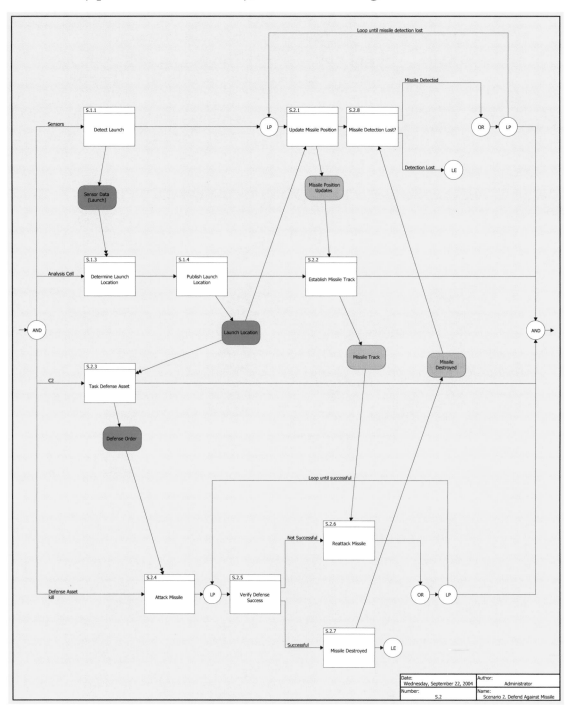

Figure 6-12. Scenario 2 EFFBD reuses Scenario 1 activities, where appropriate.

Scenario 2 reuses three of the Scenario 1 activities (Detect Launch, Determine Launch Location, and Publish Launch).

We continue to build, one scenario upon the other, until we obtain the integrated behavior discussed in the next step. But before we do, notice that with these diagrams, we immediately have our combined OV-5 and OV-6c diagram (since these are operational activities). As we dive down further, we will discover that we are defining system functions. Figure 6-13 shows an example for the Patriot defense system against multiple missile threats.

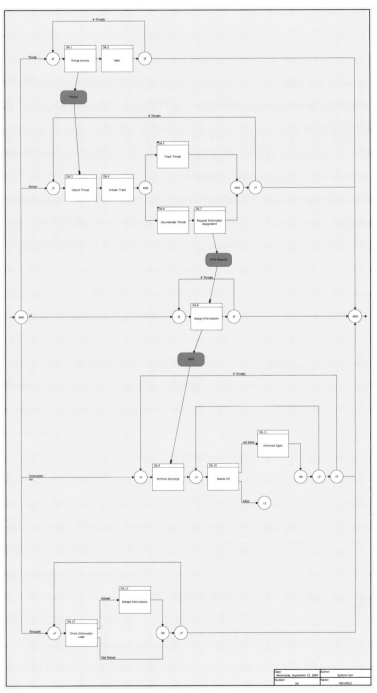

Figure 6-13. The Patriot System shows how the same analysis technique works for system functions.

Although you probably can't see the words in the boxes,[1] this diagram creates multiple threat missiles (the top line), which are detected and tracked (middle line – note how this is similar to the operational activities in the scenarios above). The third line down assigns the interceptors (as part of the C2 system), and the intercepting missiles perform their function on the fourth line down. The fifth and bottom line keeps track of the interceptors available and reloads the Patriot system when they run out.

Step 7: Derive Functional Behavior

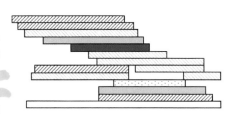

This next step brings in the art of system engineering. You must bring together the individual models developed for each scenario into a single functional behavior model. This model must still accomplish the scenarios. In fact, you can use the scenarios as test cases to verify that the integrated behavior model still works in each case.

If you deal with the scenarios in Step 6 as completely independent use cases, this step becomes very difficult. If instead you apply my suggestion, the job gets much easier. For example, when we bring together Scenario 1 and Scenario 2 to create Scenario 3 (since it clearly builds from the two previous cases), we end up with the integrated diagram shown in Figure 6-14. Now I realize you can't read the boxes in this figure any more than you could read the ones in Figure 6-13, but you can take my word that we reused all the same operational activities from Scenarios 1 & 2 and *added no additional ones for Scenario 3*. We did change the behavior of Scenarios 1 & 2 slightly in the process, but that only makes those scenarios more robust. So by continuing the scenario process outlined in Step 6, we end up with the integrated functional behavior with essentially no additional effort!

Now before you create the final set of OV-5/OV-6c and SV-4/SV-10c diagrams, you need to perform the allocations discussed in Step 9 and the abstractions of the diagrams into more readable charts.

As you progress through the decomposition, each level will be more detailed and thus take longer. Hence, you will need more time between architecture reviews at each level. Be careful to schedule major reviews at appropriate times instead of arbitrary dates; work with your customer to make sure they know right up front. Customer expectation management is part of the architect's job.

---

[1] I will apologize for these diagrams now. I know they are difficult to read, but I wanted you to get an idea of the kinds of things you can do. The specifics are not really important. To complete this job, we should abstract these diagrams to make them readable and that way have a number of levels of decomposition. Either that or an E-size plotter.

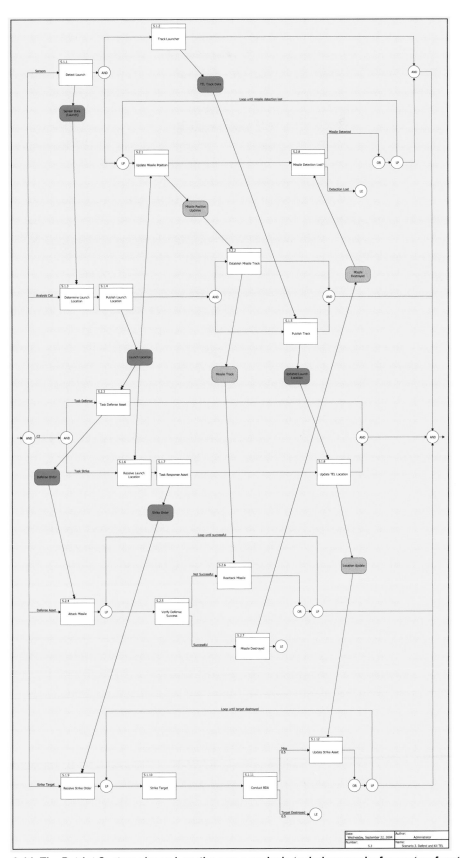

Figure 6-14. The Patriot System shows how the same analysis technique works for system functions.

Step 8: Derive System Elements

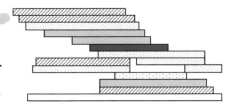

As the decomposition proceeds, you will begin to identify existing major systems (Legacy), commercial off-the-shelf (COTS) products, and Government off-the-shelf (GOTS) solutions. When you reach this point, start the functional allocation (Step 9). Likely, you will have some remaining functionality that hasn't been accomplished by the existing systems and products, at least as far as you can identify. If these functions leave a substantial gaps in the capability or pose a risk (e.g., dependency on a COTS product from a single manufacturer), you may want to begin the acquisition or prototyping process.

In determining the system elements, try to minimize the interfaces between them (i.e. if you can avoid it, don't make data pass back and forth between elements). In the new trend toward service-oriented architectures (SOA), I've seen a lot of poor packaging, and the interfaces have become very difficult to manage. The same has been true with COTS for some time and that's probably why we see the problem in SOAs as well.

The beauty of the MBSE approach is the functional requirements that you need for procurements come directly from this process. You don't have to specify a specific product or service, only the interfaces and functionality.

Step 9: Allocated Functions to System Elements

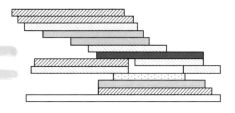

Here's were the art of system engineering comes into play

Now once we have driven the functional analysis down to the systems level, we can identify and separate the general functions into system functions and operational activities. MBSE and CORE provide relationships between these classes (*implements/implemented by*). From this information, we can generate a simple SV-5 matrix. The planner form of the SV-5 can also be developed once we have allocated system functions to systems/components and operational activities to capabilities.

In the case of the sample problem, I defined two capabilities: 1) Destroy TELs; and 2) Defend Against Missile Threats. Figure 6-15 shows a portion of the hierarchy of capabilities to operational activities to system functions. The SV-5 matrix can also be created from CORE using its report generator, but I tend to like the form shown in Figure 6-15 better. I guess to each their own. Notice that this has the same information content as the SV-5, so it would be a valid SV-5, if the customer approved.

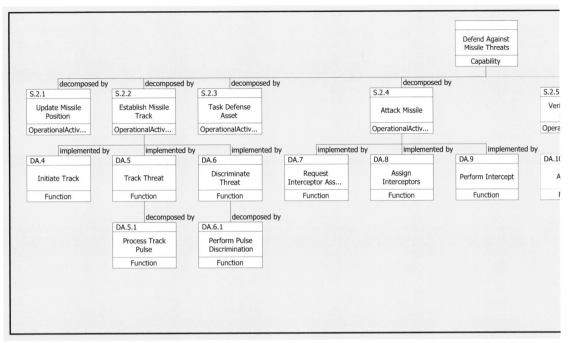

Figure 6-15. The Patriot System shows how the same analysis technique works for system functions.

Step 10: Prepare Interface Diagrams

The external interfaces are defined in the context diagram. In MBSE, the internal logical interfaces fall out of the allocation of functions (both operational activities and system functions) to components (both 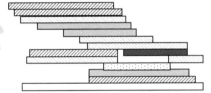 operational and system nodes). This feature results from combining the functional sequencing and the data flow in the single EFFB diagram. So when the functions are allocated to components, the data flows go along for the ride, *thus defining the data flows between components*. So the only remaining task is to determine the constraints on the means of data transmission. MBSE and CORE provide the means for capturing the capacity (e.g., bandwidth or size of the "pipe") and delay (e.g., latency). Figure 6-16 shows a text view of a link (interface) from the SV-1 shown in Figure 6-10.

The sensor link is assumed to be limited to the 400 kilobits/second given in the interface specification for Little Eye. I added the latency with a Normal distribution at a 10 millisecond (0.01 second) mean and 1 millisecond standard deviation (see the Delay attribute). We would need to validate that latency and distribution, as well as characterize the rate more accurately, but for an initial cut, it gives us some idea.

We also need to capture the information about the data items carried by the link. Figure 6-17 shows the attributes for the corresponding data element. Note how the relationships automatically point to one another, which makes finding this information much easier.

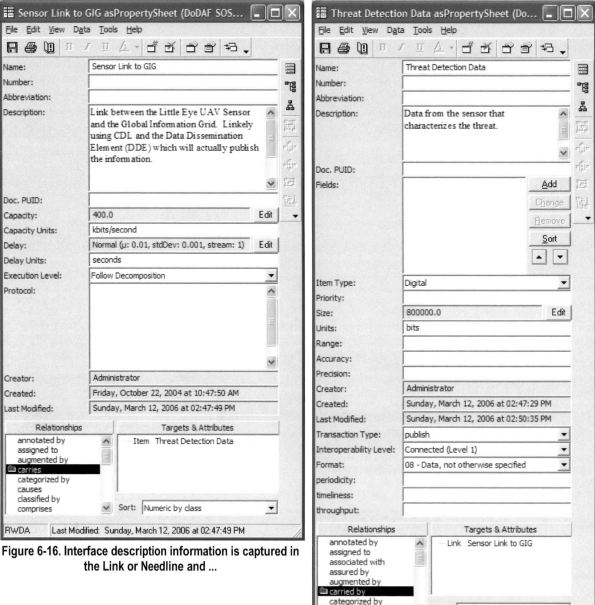

Figure 6-16. Interface description information is captured in the Link or Needline and ...

Figure 6-17. ... Item or Operational Information elements.

Clearly, we need to be sure that we fill in these attributes as we go in the analysis. I've only summarized it here, because here's the step where we produce two more of the DoDAF views: the OV-3 and SV-6.

CORE provides these two very large tables as standard reports. To print these tables in a readable form requires an 11 inch x 17 inch printer and can't be easily viewed in this book (which is why I didn't include one).

172

Step 11: Define Resources, Error Detection & Recovery

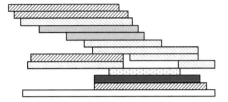

Defining the resource requirements, as well as error detection and recovery, must be done throughout the analysis; it's not something you can just add at the last minute. For example, in the Patriot model, resources have been defined in terms of the number of missiles available for each launcher (see Figure 6-18). This resource is *consumed by* two functions (*Perform Intercept* and *Intercept Again* – the Patriot system modeled uses a shoot-look-shoot scheme). Each function consumes two missiles.

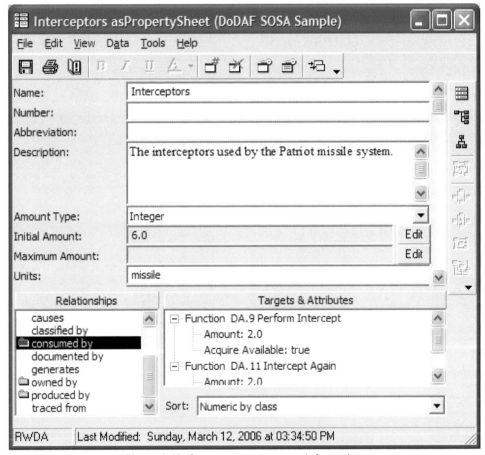

Figure 6-18. Capture your resource information.

The initial load of 6 missiles represents the Patriot capability without reloading. The reloading functions in this model are an example of "error detection and recovery." It would be an error to assume that the Patriot system wouldn't run out of missiles (this isn't an old Western), and so the correction is to detect when the resource runs out and reload the launcher.

Even in Scenario 1, I included error detection and recovery to deal with missing the target on the first strike. This scenario conducts bomb damage assessment (BDA), then orders a re-strike, and continues to update the target location, until a success has been recorded. In Scenario 2, I included the possibility of losing the missile track during the defensive engagement. So you can see that by including realistic problems and resource constraints as part of your scenarios, it makes this step fairly easy.

Step 12: Perform Dynamic Analysis

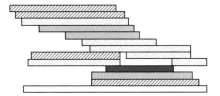

This step also needs to be done throughout the functional analysis. You can execute the EFFBDs (in both the *Operational Activity* and *Function* classes). You should run the simulator for each of the scenarios in the early stages just to verify the logic. In later stages, you can use it to predict the performance of the system under the realistic constraints imposed by resource limitations, sizes of data elements, bandwidth, and latency.

Figure 6-19 shows the simulator results for the Patriot model. You can see the red bars indicating that the system ran out of missiles and computer power (MIPS), as well as, the impacts on the timeline of those constraints.

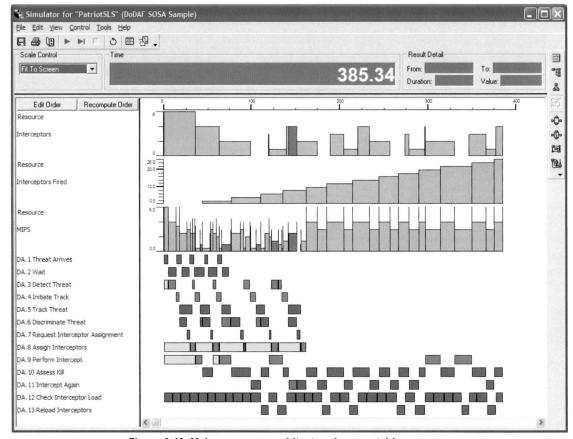

Figure 6-19. Make sure your architecture is executable.

Clearly, since the interceptor keeps running out of missiles, we may need two batteries to deal with the threat level postulated. We would also want to upgrade the computer system to a faster processor. These kinds of insights make great *Findings* for the AV-1 and are just the kind of information decision makers need. To facilitate the capture of Findings, I extended the CORE schema to add that class. Figure 6-20 shows this finding and traces it back to the simulation model where the problem was discovered. Capturing these findings as you go through the process will save a lot of time later when some asks: "So where did you get that from?"

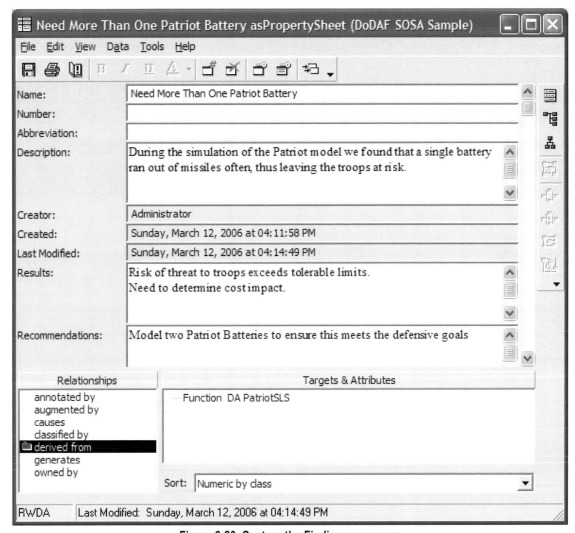

Figure 6-20. Capture the Findings as you go.

Step 13: Develop Operational Demonstration Master Plan

A lot of people would tell you that this step is out of scope for an architecture study. In fact, I think this is one of the most critical steps. We all need to consider how the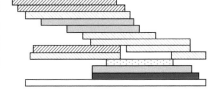

architecture will ultimately be acceptable and transitioned into operations. An operational demonstration could be part of an advanced concept technology demonstration (ACTD) or joint experimentation (such as JWID) project. Or you could just be getting ready for buy off at the end of an ACAT I acquisition lifecycle, where you have a full scale operational test and evaluation (OT&E). But the time to start thinking and planning for the verification of your architecture's capabilities is during the architecture development.

Fortunately, MBSE and CORE make that process somewhat easier with an entire facility devoted to verification. Figure 6-21 shows the verification facility elements (far left panel) and a table view of the *VerificationRequirement* class elements developed for this sample problem. This class allows you to consider different *techniques* for verifying the requirement, including simulation, demonstration, and test (as shown in the figure).

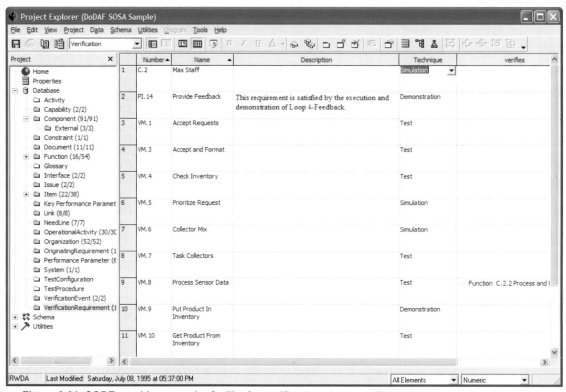

Figure 6-21. CORE provides an entire facility for verification elements (Table View shown here).

CORE also provides a test and evaluation plan report to document the results of these analyses and prepare for the development of a complete master plan. Remember that you can tailor this report like any other to include external graphics and elements, relationships, and attributes that you define.

Step 14: Provide Options

At the end of the architecture project, you will need to present the results of trade studies (see next step), findings, and architecture products. Make sure you've captured and summarized all the options available, including ones that might have 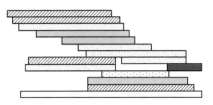 been pursued if certain decisions hadn't been made. Your customers will be much happier if you can provide them with options, but in *lieu* of having specific options at the end, they should be satisfied that they were "in-the-loop" all the way through the project.

Make sure you consider who you will be presenting the architecture to and try to use their language, so they will understand and feel comfortable with the results. Chapter 7 discusses this point is more detail.

Step 15: Conduct Trade-off Studies

The last two steps actually can occur throughout the project (even though I show this one starting more in the middle). Remember to make the trade-off studies explicit, not just in your head. Many of the issues that get brought up early and often 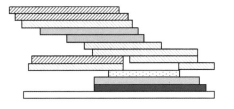 throughout this process will result in some form of trade study to resolve them. Capture the results of those trade-offs as you go. Make sure you keep the customer involved in the development of the evaluation criteria and results.

Step 16: Generate Views Graphics, Briefings and Reports

This last step clearly occurs throughout the process. At any point in time, your customer may need information on the status of the project and any preliminary results. Here's where the tool comes in to save you. CORE 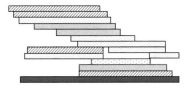 provides a large set of standard reports (see Figure 6-22 for the list). a powerful scripting language, and reporting facility.

Many of the scripts are already designed to include the external text and graphics you have provided. Note that the graphics must be in a JPEG or other graphics form that Microsoft Word recognizes for publication and in rich text format (RTF) or comma separated values (CSV) formats.

I have created a number of special reports (some of which show up in the list in Figure 6-22). I've even used the tool to capture processes and create procedure documentation, with icons, headers and footers, and automatic tables of contents. So there's not much you can't do with the report generator. It should more than meet your specific needs.

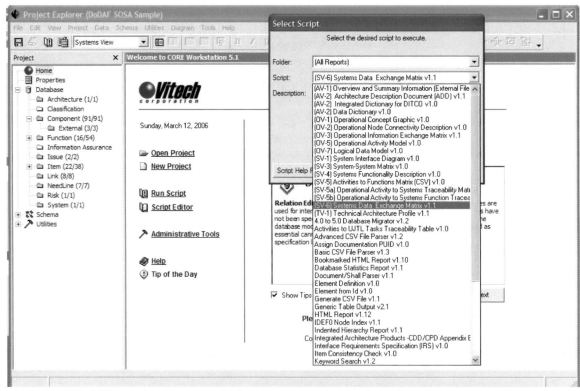

Figure 6-22. CORE provides many standard reports and a robust scripting language to create your own.

Sample Problem Wrap-Up

I hope you found this walk though my sample problem helpful in developing your methodology. You will probably see things you like and things you don't. But please remember, the process described above heavily depends on the technique (Model-Based System Engineering) and the Tool (CORE). If you plan to use another tool or technique, please develop an appropriate process.

Now on to the final chapter; and in it, we will discuss some things I hope I've "foot stomped" all the way through the rest of the book: 1) you must communicate with your customers all throughout the project; and 2) architecture is all about communication.

7

How Can We Communicate the Results Better?

In this final chapter, we will look at how architectures can enhance the communication between the different stakeholders of the potential development. Although I have made some of these points throughout the book, I'd like to now focus on ways you can better communicate the results of your work, thus improving the acceptance of the results and enabling others to get what they need out of all your hard work.

First, I'd like to consider the different things you can do in the development of architecture products that will enhance communication. One of the things you can do is create or obtain from any reviewers the evaluation criteria that they will use to judge the success of the project. Some of these criteria will be explicit, provided to you in a statement of work or some other contractual means. If they are well-defined and agreed upon up front by both parties (and the people don't change during the project, which can then throw off the whole thing), meeting those criteria should be relatively straight forward.

Other criteria will be more informal. The perceptions different stakeholders will have of the architecture will cause you more problems than the explicit criteria. Different people will read and interpret the explicit criteria in different ways, as well as have other criteria or standards of which they aren't necessarily even aware. As part of your requirements analysis process, make sure you talk (directly if possible) to the stakeholders to gauge what they think is needed. Try to capture and resolve issues as early in the process as possible. That way, you will at least know what each individual's concerns are, and you can show them how you've tried to fix any perceived problems. Make sure as new people come on-board that you have a history file (here's where that *Issue/Decision* report from CORE can come in handy) for them to review and come up to speed.

Another thing you can do is use automated tools and databases to be able to answer the "what-if" questions quickly. If you're stuck in what I call "paper mode," where you treat everything as a document, then you miss out on the power of automation and a database. The tools need to help you, not be a burden. One of the reasons I chose CORE was its schema automatically established the reverse relationships between elements. This means that I can navigate up or down the relationships to find the elements related to it, quickly and easily. Most tools do not provide the visibility into the schema or a schema extension facility that lets you rapidly capture any information needed to answer questions. CORE does. Make sure if your tool has these features, you become familiar with them so you can be Mr. or Ms. Answer.

Another clear tool capability you need is simulators. Many tools have them embedded now. They let you and your customer see the time dimension (and often other variables) and its effect on performance.

The last of the "things you can do" is to use the standards, such as the Universal Joint Task List (UJTL), Net Centric Operations and Warfare (NCOW) Reference Model, and the DoD Enterprise Architecture Reference Models, as a starting point for your analysis. By using these as operational activities or other architecture elements, you almost can guarantee that your audience won't complain about your starting assumptions. Plus, your audience will likely be familiar with them, so you start from a common basis of understanding, which is a clear benefit for communication. Likewise, use the technical standards from the Joint Technical Architecture/DISRonline. Finally, use other commercial standards, including ones for methodology, as much as possible to provide comfort to those reviewing your work that you haven't been "reinventing the wheel."

Now let's talk about how we can introduce the changes to the organizations and people affected by architectures. *Change Management* can enhance both the communication of the architecture results and the acceptance of the changes they bring.

What Role Does Change Management Play in Architecture Development?

Change Management is the process of managing change by communicating the benefits (and costs if not adopted) of change. Architectures imply change, which causes concern among the staff that will be affected by the change. The key to change management is communication, communication, and more communication.

Now you may be wondering how this affects you as an architect. All architectures are about change. You will be changing the way someone does business, if you impact their operations. You change the way people do their job, if you give them new tools. You will affect their work environment, if you are changing their organization. Hence, all architecture is about change. So what can we expect for people, when confronted with change? Let's start with understanding why they resist change, then we will look at the reactions to change, and finally how to deal with perceptions of the change the issues, real and imagined, that result.

Why Do People Resist Change? Often it's a combination of fear, insecurity, and uncertainty. People are afraid of what changes will bring them or even threatened by the perceived as well as the real changes. They may not even be sure of what they are afraid of or threatened by: loss of job, prestige, or position. Change make people feel insecure and uncertain; since they don't know what's going to happen, they imagine the worst.

Another reason people resist change comes from a feeling that there is no compelling reason to change. I remember one of the first things I heard when I worked at Los Alamos National Laboratory, "If it ain't broke, don't fix it." It didn't matter that it was going to break tomorrow or that the current method was inefficient. Sometimes people near a situation don't see the problems looming. These problems can cause the very things they are afraid of for themselves and perhaps the entire organization.

How do people react to change? Figure 7-1 demonstrates that for people to accept change they must perceive it as is going from a current state of "pain" (or ineffectiveness, non-profitability, etc.) through a transitional state to get to the future state where the remedy to the pain has been implemented. This concept isn't that abstract. You can think of this as you have a current "As-Is" architecture, where you have serious operational gaps that cause you to loose troops in combat, such as the improvised explosive devices (IED) in Iraq. It's a daily problem (in March 2006), but one you can't put a major force against. We need an immediate solution to the problem, but we also need a long term solution. They could enhance these devices to make them more lethal by adding other technologies; hence, a "To-Be" architecture will be critical in the long term.

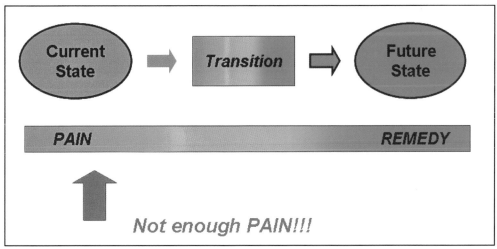

Figure 7-1. Sometime you have to add a little pain to make the change.

In a situation like this, you may find people "dragging their feet" on either a short term or long term solution, because it interferes with their current operations and plans or comfort level. Harsh as it may seem, here's where the management would have to come in and add a little pain, such as demotions or some other form of punishment to make an example out a recalcitrant. In this way, more people will realize that the change is necessary.

You may receive a number of reactions to change from individuals over time. The reaction often goes through phases of shock ("Where did this come from?"), anger ("It won't work!"), denial ("Don't blame me!"), and finally acceptance ("Let's get on with it.") Part of the change manager's job is to help people through these phases by communicating what's going on, and why it will benefit them and the rest of the organization. As the architect, you may also have to play the role of the change manager, so don't be surprised.

One thing that might help you as the change manager is to recognize that people tend to fall into three categories: *casualties, pioneers,* and *survivors.* The *casualties* feel threatened and will be cynical about the success of the change. They may even undermine the change by talking badly about the change to other employees or drag their feet on implementation. The other extreme is the *pioneer,* they are people who embrace change and see the opportunities that change brings. They understand the temporary pain change brings with it and accept it as the cost of doing business. The *survivors* are initially fearful, but will ultimately accept the change because they want to be on the winning side, which means this is the group you will have to work at first to sway to the side of change. They're the swing voters in this election.

I use an election analogy here, because just like the electorate, about a third are casualties, another third are pioneers, and the final third are survivors. Even in the U.S. Senate, a 2/3 majority can defeat a filibuster. Now I know that a lot of you will think, "Well management can just direct the change to happen and it will happen." Those of you who think that quote is right haven't been working for any of the organizations that I know. To move forward on anything, you need to have the people who will implement on the side of change, or it won't happen. They will just wait out the initial barrage of the change agents, hoping they will move on. And usually they are right! So the key to a successful change is to move as many people as possible toward acceptance of the change.

You can spot acceptance in the questions that team members will ask. As they begin, the questions will be all about themselves:

- What is this change?
- How will it affect me and my job?
- How will I be evaluated?

As they progress toward acceptance, the questions become more focused on the change itself:

- How will this change be carried out?
- What are the benefits?

- What will the overall impact be?

Finally, when they are accepting the change, you will be asked questions about how they can help with the change:

- How can I help others?
- How can we implement improvements?

Frequent Issues: Perceived and Real. Some of the issues that you will face (and remember to most people perception is reality) include:

1. Actions intended to increase understanding and trust often produces misunderstanding and distrust
2. Blaming others or the system for own poor decisions
3. Organizational inertia
4. Lack of upward communication for difficult issues
5. Budget games
6. Irrational behavior
7. No real management "team"

You may not expect some of these issues; although if you've been in the business for sometime, you've probably seen them all and more. Before you try to implement change, in the form of the new CONOPS or systems or organization derived from the architecture, be sure you consider these factors and develop a workable plan to overcome or at least reduce the impact of these issues.

To fully implement change, you need to understand the people to whom you will be presenting the architectural changes. Let's discuss the target audience and what motivates them.

Who Is My Target Audience?

Your target audience will consist of a variety of different kinds of people, from end users to developers and from to acquisition personnel to warfighters. Recognize that you may have to tailor individual products for different audiences, and most will not understand any of the DoDAF products, except the OV-1, which they may not even like.

Let me give you an example. I had a project where we were developing an architecture for a research and development organization that wanted to improve their acquisition approach to better align it with the DoD budget cycle. In the process of performing this study, a new officer came on board to oversee the project. This officer, an Air Force O-6, wasn't a system engineer and didn't feel he understood the diagrams we were developing, an example of which is shown in Figure 7-2. Once I realized this, I decided to re-draw the executable diagrams in Microsoft PowerPoint. That required a little thought, because you can easily draw the diagram in ways that doesn't express the parallel nature of the EFFBD shown. I needed to be sure that he could see that these three functions were occurring simultaneously, for different data sets. If I had drawn the diagram as a sequence or waterfall, that critical point would be lost.

As drawn, the two diagrams carry the same meaning, but the PowerPoint diagram can not be easily tested (executed) and the EFFBD can. I took an entire day to redraw the resulting diagrams, and my customer was happy. He felt he understood what he was seeing, and in fact, asked pertinent questions about the architecture. So it was worth the person-day. My new customer became an advocate for the architecture work.

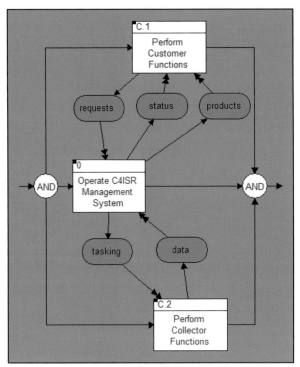

Figure 7-2. A typical EFFBD

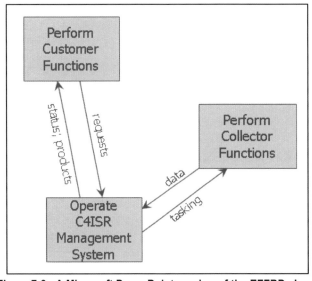

Figure 7-3. A Microsoft PowerPoint version of the EFFBD above

So what questions might your target audience ask? They may ask: "How does this help me understand the architecture better?" This person is trying to understanding how the DoDAF products describe the architecture in a meaningful way. After all, the DoDAF products represent a *model* of the architecture, not the real architecture as it will finally be implemented.

Another question you might face is, "How does this help me make a decision?" Decision makers expect the architecture and its products to help them solve problems, such as when to invest in which technologies, or how to reorganize to better achieve a new mission or goal.

The acquisition personnel might ask, "How does this help me get the best bang for the buck?" They are the stewards of the taxpayer dollars and should be interested in the value the architecture provides in keeping costs reasonable. After all, the Government just invested a healthy chunk of money in the architecture study, instead of somewhere else. It better have been money well spent.

The patriot in the group will ask, "How does this enhance national security?" That person understands that DoD's primary role is to safeguard the country and wants to ensure that any architectural changes meet that objective, as should we all.

Finally, you may encounter the realist (I have) who asks, "How does this get me my next promotion?" You may laugh at this one (I usually get a few chuckles in the audience when I mention it), but as a contractor, I understand what the person is saying. Our job as contractors is to help our Government counterparts achieve what is important to them. Sometimes, this is more advanced rank. If you do so, it's a win-win-win. The Government person wins by achieving a personal goal, the contractor wins, because now the Government customer knows who to choose for the next (bigger) project, and the country wins, because the architecture was seen as a success by the superiors who promoted the Government customer.

You will likely run into all these people at one point or another. These are their real evaluation criteria. You need to be able to understand what motivates these individuals so you can better communicate the results of the architecture development.

One thing that everyone concerned with the architecture needs to know is how the architecture provides value. I found that by applying some form of standard approach to this helps the communications process. One of the recent "standards" adopted by the General Accounting Office (GAO) is "Balanced Scorecard."[1] Balanced Scorecard is an approach to provide decision makers with a way to make investment strategy decisions. It is currently required by the GAO for each

---

[1] GAO Report GAO/AIMD-98-89, "Measuring Performance and Demonstrating Results of Information Technology Investments"

Department and Agency in the Government at that very high level. But it is also useful at lower levels of decision making.

Balanced Scorecard has three major steps:

Step 1. Define Mission and Desired Outcomes

Step 2. Measure Performance Practices

Step 3. Use Performance Information

I converted this approach to the table format shown in Figure 7-4. The first column of this table provides the evaluation criteria. The categories of criteria include cost, risk (Concept/Technology Maturity), schedule, and performance – the basic foci of systems engineering. The next column shows the key or most important function requirements in those categories (hence the detailed evaluation criteria), the baseline (or "As-Is") value or ranking of the "As-Is" concept or program element, and alternative concepts and elements for a decision maker to select.

Concept/Program Element:

Evaluation Criteria	Key Functional Requirements	Baseline	Proposed Concepts/ Elements		
Cost					
Concept/ Technology Maturity					
Schedule for Implementation					
Performance					

Figure 7-4. A simple chart communicates well to decision makers.

By using alternative architecture products like this, you can enhance the communications with a wider variety of evaluators and customers. Use every trick in the book and don't feel constrained by the DoDAF products.

Summary

Hopefully, you have learned a lot from this book. The lessons in it come from hard experience. But before we finish, we need to address one more topic. Where is the DoDAF going? Will it be characterized by stimulating architectural *rigor* or result in *rigor mortis* to the process? I bring up this question with DoDAF 2.0 looming out there, because the changes that this new version will make will help answer this question. Like everything else in life there are people who love the DoDAF and what it does and others who hate it and what it represents (lack of "flexibility" or in other words, "I can't do it my way, so I don't want to play.")

I think I've shown you how flexible the DoDAF really is, but that flexibility depends on the reviewer, the customer, or some other recipient of the architecture. Let's be clear, the DoDAF is mandatory policy, as the letter in Figure 7-5 shows.

OFFICE OF THE SECRETARY OF DEFENSE
WASHINGTON, DC 20301

FEB 9 2004

MEMORANDUM FOR SECRETARIES OF THE MILITARY DEPARTMENTS
    CHAIRMAN OF THE JOINT CHIEFS OF STAFF
    UNDER SECRETARIES OF DEFENSE
    COMBATANT COMMANDERS
    ASSISTANT SECRETARIES OF DEFENSE
    GENERAL COUNSEL OF THE DEPARTMENT OF DEFENSE
    INSPECTOR GENERAL OF THE DEPARTMENT OF DEFENSE
    DIRECTOR, OPERATIONAL TEST AND EVALUATION
    DIRECTOR, ADMINISTRATION AND MANAGEMENT
    DIRECTOR, PROGRAM ANALYSIS AND EVALUATION
    DIRECTOR OF NET ASSESSMENT
    DIRECTOR, FORCE TRANSFORMATION
    DIRECTORS OF DEFENSE AGENCIES

SUBJECT: The Department of Defense Architecture Framework (DoDAF)

The DoD Architecture Framework (DoDAF) Version 1.0 is approved for immediate use. All architectures developed or approved subsequent to December 1, 2003, shall be in compliance with this framework. Architectures developed prior to this date shall be converted upon issuance of their next version update.

John P Stenbit

John P. Stenbit
Department of Defense
Chief Information Officer

Figure 7-5. DoDAF has been mandated, but will we care?

But those of us who've worked in and around DoD for a long time know that you can wait out policies that don't make sense or aren't useful to those of us who must implement them. How many of you remember Ada? It was the "official DoD programming language" mandated in the early 1990s. And how many of you program in that language today? People obtained waiver's, worked around it by having Ada shells call C and Fortran code, or just ignored it. It went away.

I would hate to see the same thing happen to the DoDAF. Why? Because we need it or something similar to it. The DoDAF is useful to us because it provides a standard for communicating the essential elements of architectures. It can support the *justification and defense* of your program funding, but it also fosters interoperability, which is essential in saving the lives of our service men and women and making our fighting forces more effective. The DoDAF links the higher-level concepts and capabilities with detailed implementation, forming a bridge between concept and detailed design. Finally, one of my favorite reasons is that it makes the case for an executable system engineering approach, not just viewgraph engineering.

If we don't adopt DoDAF, we would have to reinvent it, which is a great time and expense. We need to work with OSD/NII and help them keep it flexible enough to remain a useful tool. As architects, we owe it to our customer to help them by providing executable architectures, i.e. ones that work.

What I'd like you to take away from this book is how to put together an effective architecture. You need to:

- Do the systems engineering right, then produce any required documentation (e.g. DoDAF Views)
- Summarize the results in an easy to read section, then provide detail in appendices
- Provide a simple briefing that focuses on the findings, not how you got there
- You will need the "how you got there" to back up the findings

The key decisions you need to make are: 1) to select a proven technique; 2) obtain a set of easy-to-use, integrated tools that support the technique; and 3) develop a tailored architecture and system design process. With these three points, you will have gone a long way toward developed an executable methodology to make your next architecture study a success.

Remember: Good systems engineering provides your methodology... DoDAF products give you the way to communicate your results.

Good Luck on your next architecture project.

Author's Acknowledgments

I would like to thank my editors, Robin Viar and Rebecca Dam, for all their help in trying to keep this poor physicist's grammar correct. I also want to thank Scott Dam again for the back cover photograph of me. Helen Kouts came on board to SPEC recently and did an incredible job of putting together the cover in a matter of days.

Special thanks go to Jim Willis for his last minute "peer review," taking precious time away from his limited home life.

I would also like to thank Jim and David Long of Vitech Corporation for their many hours of instruction on Model-Based System Engineering and allowing us to use their material in this book.

Thanks also belong to the men and women who have come to our DoDAF training courses and contributed their thoughts and ideas along the way.

I also want to express my appreciation to the dedicated OSD, MITRE and contractor personnel who developed the DoDAF and the other documents and briefing materials shown in this book. They daily contribute to the body of knowledge in architecture and system engineering without which any book like this would be impossible to write.

Lastly, but not least, I want to thank my wife (and boss in everyway) Cindy and our kids (Rebecca and Elizabeth) for their patience with "Dad's writing another book!" Two in two years can put a lot of stress on a home life. I couldn't do it without them.

Made in the USA